# SHOT D!

*When his bomber exploded over Nazi-occupied France,*
*only John survived—and found a new life*

# John M. Curnow

**Pacific Press® Publishing Association**
Nampa, Idaho
Oshawa, Ontario, Canada
www.pacificpress.com

Designed by Dennis Ferree
Cover photos provided by author

Additional copies of this book are available by calling toll free 1-800-765-6955
or
by visiting www.adventistbookcenter.com


Library of Congress Cataloging-in-Publication Data

Curnow, John M. (John Maurice), 1923-
Shot down! : when his bomber explodes over Nazi-occupied France, only John
survives—and finds a new life/John M. Curnow.
p. cm.
ISBN: 0-8163-2109-4
ISBN 13: 9780816321094
1. Curnow, John M. (John Maurice), 1923- 2. World War, 1939–1945—Aerial
operations, British. 3. World War, 1939–1945—Prisoners and prisions,
German. 4. World War, 1939–1945—Personal narratives, British.
5. Great Britain. Royal Air Force—Biography. 6. Prisoners of war—Germany—
Biography. 7. Prisoners of war—Great Britain—Biography. 8. Bomber pilots—
Great Britain—Biography. 9. Christian life. I. Title

D805.G3C85 2006
940.54'214'092—dc22
[B]                                                    2005049264


08 09 10 11 · 5 4 3 2

# DEDICATED

to the memory of my crew:

*Royal Air Force*
*Lancaster Mk 1, PM-D, W4860*
*103rd Squadron*
*Shot down March 10, 1943*

*John Victor Roper*
Pilot

*John Alexander Todd*
Bomb Aimer

*Stanley John Rose*
Flight Engineer

*John Scott Dobie*
Wireless Operator

*Jack (John) Smith*
Mid-Upper Gunner

*Ernest Solomon Waghorn*
Rear Gunner

and all Allied airmen of World War II, who gave their all for the freedom of their beloved homelands and the liberation of Europe and the Far East.

And to the *Voice of Prophecy* which, through the ministries of H. M. S. Richards, Sr., the King's Heralds, and Del Delker, helped me become a Christian when, in 1952, I accepted Jesus Christ as my personal Savior.

# ACKNOWLEDGMENTS

My thanks go first to my friend, Tony Muse, whose discovery of a French Web site led to my decision to write this sequel to *Death on Dark Wings,* an account of my wartime experiences, authored by Thomas A. Davis and published in 1973.

I also profoundly thank Olivier Housseaux, whose Web site led me to the grave site of my crew at Lavannes, France, and then to the Web site of the association of my old 103rd Squadron in England.

I am also indebted to David W. Fell, Internet secretary of the association, whose extensive knowledge and databases of the squadron's wartime records have provided much accurate and enriching material for this book.

I extend my deep appreciation to Thomas Davis, author of *Death on Dark Wings* and numerous other books and articles, for reading the original manuscript, suggesting improvements, and offering valuable advice. I want to thank Mrs. Edith Willis, assistant professor, Southwestern Adventist University, for proofreading. And my heartfelt thanks to my wife, Joan, without whose encouragement and patience as I spent many hours at the computer to the neglect of other responsibilities, this book would not have been written. Also my thanks to my daughter Dr. Sally Anne Mashburn, who spent many hours organizing into chronological order all my wartime letters which my mother had kept, along with the handwritten copies of the letters my mother had written to me. These old letters have provided priceless, and otherwise long forgotten, information.

Above all, I want to thank God for bringing me alive from that doomed plane as it plummeted to earth and for guiding me in so many wondrous ways ever since.

# CONTENTS

# PREFACE

Stunned, I sat in front of my computer monitor, staring at the picture of six gravestones, each bearing the insignia of the Royal Air Force. Deep emotions began to well up within my heart. Slowly I scrolled from one close-up picture to the next—John Dobie, Jack Smith, John Roper, Ernest Waghorn, John Todd, and Stanley John Rose. On the headstones were engraved short messages from loved ones. On the headstone of John Todd, my bomb aimer, his wife had had engraved:

FROM TWILIGHT
TO THE HALLS OF DAWN HE WENT.
HIS LANCE IS BROKEN,
BUT HE LIES CONTENT.

When I read those words I broke down and cried. For the first time in sixty years I truly grieved the loss of my six friends and crew members. When we were shot down I had been sorry they had been killed, but preoccupation with trying to escape, and then being captured, had left no time for real grieving.

As I looked at the photos, I knew I had to go to that church graveyard in the village of Lavannes, France.

A young friend of mine, Tony Muse, saw a Lancaster bomber model kit on eBay. Knowing I had flown on the Lancaster in World War II, he bid for it so he could model it for me. When it came time for the decals, he wanted to use the letters and numbers of my old squadron. Going to an Internet search engine he entered my name, followed by "Royal Air Force." This took him to Olivier Housseaux's French Web site.

Housseaux had dedicated his Web site to keeping alive the memory of Allied airmen shot down and killed over his county in France. He knew about my crew, for they were buried only eight miles from the city of Reims where he lived. Knowing there had been a lone survivor, he had written on one of his Web site pages, "I am looking for J. M. Curnow."

Thanks to Tony Muse, Housseaux has at last found me, and I have found my crew!

# NO TURNING BACK!

The poster jumped out at me, grabbing my attention! I sat in the train on my way to school in London, my eyes riveted to the image of a young Royal Air Force pilot, his outstretched arm and finger pointing straight at me, his piercing eyes boring into mine. Underneath the picture, in bold type and capital letters, I read: YOUR COUNTRY NEEDS YOU—JOIN THE ROYAL AIR FORCE!

I felt my heart pounding in my chest. A small voice within me was saying, "Do what Norman has done. Do what Norman has done." Norman Howard was my best friend. We had grown up together in the picturesque village of Ickenham situated about twelve miles west of London.

Some two months earlier I had bumped into Norman in Ickenham. Excitedly, he had exclaimed, "John, guess what! I've just joined the RAF to train as a pilot!"

Surprised, I responded, "How did you do that? You're not old enough." I knew he had only recently turned seventeen and that the minimum age for volunteering was eighteen.

He grinned and waved his hand nonchalantly. "I put my age up. I told them I was eighteen!"

My admiring eyes had followed him as he hurried on his way. In a few weeks I would be seventeen, too. What if I . . . ?

The year was 1940. The "Phony War," as it had been called, had come to a violent and sudden end earlier that year, as the Germans launched their blitzkrieg on the Western Front. Smashing through

*The old St. Giles Church, Ickenham village*

Belgium and Holland at bewildering speed, German Panzer divisions had been able to drive deep into France. The French were completely unprepared for such a lightning advance. Resistance collapsed, and France was forced to sue for peace.

The British army that had gone to bolster the French forces was outflanked, but managed to make a fighting retreat to the French coast. There, at the famous Battle of Dunkirk, a thin line of gallant British soldiers kept the enemy at bay while more than three hundred thousand of their comrades were snatched from the blood-stained North Sea beaches and from certain imprisonment. Defying enemy U-boats and the German *Luftwaffe*, hundreds of ships and boats, large and small, military and civilian, plowed back and forth across the forty-five miles of dangerous waters separating England from France and successfully ferried the British soldiers back to England.

The bulk of the British Expeditionary Force was now safely back in its homeland. But it was an army without weapons, for all arms and equipment had to be abandoned in the evacuation. Britain, with its back to the wall, was virtually defenseless except for its fighter planes patrolling the skies and its navy dominating the seas separating it from what was now Nazi-controlled Europe. Would proud England, which had not been invaded for nearly a thousand years, survive?

These were truly England's darkest days! But our new leader, Winston Churchill, in a mighty speech to the nation, lifted us out of despondency and filled our hearts with a determination to fight back and win. It was at this time that I joined the Home Guard, a volunteer paramilitary force of civilians made up mostly of men too old for the regular military, but also including a few teenagers like myself who were too young to enlist. It was one of Britain's lines of defense against a German paratroop invasion.

The uneasy calm was shattered one sunny day in August 1940 as Hitler launched his vaunted *Luftwaffe* against England in an all-out attempt to gain mastery of the skies over our green and pleasant land. The air war was intended to prepare for a ground invasion. In what was to become known as the Battle of Britain, hundreds of Messerschmitt 109 and 110 fighters and many Dornier, Heinkel, and Junkers bombers swept over the English Channel in an endeavor to destroy the Royal Air Force both in the air and on the ground. But Hitler was to lose the Battle of Britain with very heavy losses as RAF Hurricane and Spitfire fighters rose to shoot down hundreds of the enemy's planes.

The valor of those gallant fighter pilots was etched into my mind as I listened to the daily reports of this epic struggle. One Hurricane pilot was shot down twice in one day! Both times he landed safely by parachute and commandeered a car to get back to his aerodrome and take off once more in another Hurricane to do battle with the enemy! The sacrificial gallantry of these brave pilots was immortalized by Churchill's tribute: "Never in the field of human conflict was so much owed by so many to so few."

Failing in his daylight attacks, Hitler turned to nightly bombing of my beloved London. Night after night, while on Home Guard duty in Ickenham, I would watch the eastern sky turn red as the fires raged from the bombing. I became bitterly angry and wanted revenge.

The Battle of Britain, 1940. "Never . . . was so much owed by so many to so few."—Winston Churchill.

Now as I sat in that train, my eyes riveted on the poster and its challenge, YOUR COUNTRY NEEDS YOU—JOIN THE ROYAL AIR FORCE!, I was about to make my fateful decision. One of the recruiting centers listed on the poster was in the town of

*My beloved London under attack. This was a challenge I had to meet!*

Acton, the very next station! As the train came to a stop and the doors opened, my eyes went to the station name on the platform, then back to the poster. Again, my glance went from the station name and back to the poster.

With heart thumping, I bounded onto the platform just as the doors closed behind me and the train went on its way.

I located the recruiting center, took a deep breath, and strode inside. The recruiting sergeant looked at me enquiringly. I told him I had come to join the RAF.

"How old are you?" he asked, no doubt because of my boyish face.

"Eighteen," I answered defiantly, daring him to challenge me.

Was it my imagination or did I see his eyes narrow a little as he pushed an application form across the desk to me? Quickly filling out the form, I signed it and pushed it back to him. As he took it, I knew a bridge had been crossed; there was no turning back now!

# BOOT CAMP AND BEYOND

I left the recruiting office feeling elated and excited—but also a little apprehensive. I wondered how my parents would respond. Returning to the station, I got on the next train and continued my journey to school. There, I explained why I was late and that it would be my last day to attend classes.

Later that evening I plucked up courage to tell my parents what I had done. A look of alarm came over my mother's face. My father's lips pressed tightly together, and his brow furrowed. He nodded his head slightly. He commuted every day to London, where he worked in a bank, and he knew better than I did what our great city was enduring night after night from Hitler's bombs. And he, himself, had fought on the battlefields of Flanders in World War I only twenty-two years earlier. When I made my announcement, he said quietly, "Yes, this great evil has to be fought. God be with you, my son."

For several days I waited impatiently for a letter from the Air Ministry. Why was it taking so long? Finally the letter arrived. It instructed me to report to an RAF center in London for physical and written examinations. With pent-up excitement I reported to the center on September 19, 1940.

After the examinations, an officer interviewed me and advised me I should train as an observer rather than as a pilot because of my strong showing in the mathematics test. An observer was both a navigator and a bombardier. He further told me that I would be able to start training immediately as an observer. Since the pay and categories of rank were the same for both pilots and observers, I decided to follow the officer's advice. Taking the oath of allegiance, I enlisted in the Royal Air Force Volunteer Reserve! I received instructions to report immediately for basic training at the Winslow RAF Station near Manchester.

My life took a dramatic turn as soon as I arrived at boot camp. I was issued uniforms, a gas mask, and other service gear, and the process of turning raw civilians into military men began without delay. How well I remember bayonet practice! With blood-curdling yells, we violently jabbed our bayonets into stuffed dummies! The foot drill was not new to me as I had already learned that in the Officer Training Corps that my school had operated.

One thing that broke the monotony of boot camp was the keen competition between the numerous barracks; each group of recruits strove to have the best record for spick-and-span neatness by the end of the six-week course. My group was determined to be the unit that would receive the commanding officer's commendation. No detail was considered too insignificant to be overlooked. Prior to the official daily inspection, we checked our beds for precise alignment, double-checked our lockers to see that everything conformed to the required order and layout of its contents. We made sure to keep the windows spotless, both inside and out (with no Windex to help us!), and we polished the floor until it reflected light like a mirror.

But we went even further. We selected uniform-sized pieces of coal from the coal box and polished them with shoe polish so they sparkled like huge black diamonds. We carefully kept these to one side when the stove was being used. Then just in time for the inspection, we put them back in the coal box on top of the rest of the coal! But I think the ultimate in our spick-and-span regimen was scraping the broom handles with razor blades so that they looked like new. That was my task.

At the end of the six weeks, our barrack won the inspection!

But, for me, boot camp also ended with a big disappointment. I had keenly anticipated starting my training as an observer at the end of boot camp. Hadn't I been told that would be the case?

Instead I was posted to Drem, an airbase for a squadron of Hurricane fighters, located in a bleak, windswept corner of southeast Scotland. Drem was one of the "rest" airfields. Each fighter squadron rotated between three locations: the front line airfields in the main battle zone of southern England; intermediate airfields located where there was less enemy activity; and "rest" airfields, where battle-weary pilots could recuperate. These "rest" airfields were usually located up north in Scotland where there was little or no enemy activity.

The RAF station at Drem was a unique place—at least the squadron commander was unique! Wing Commander "Batty" Acherly had gotten his nickname because of his reputation of sometimes being a little crazy when in the air. But at the same time he was highly respected as one of the best fighter aces from the Battle of Britain.

At the intermediate airfield where Acherly's squadron had been stationed, the control tower was very close to another building; the space between them was barely two feet wider than the wingspan of a Hurricane fighter plane. The story was that "Batty" Acherly would sometimes dive his Hurricane through that narrow space with only inches to spare on either side! Other pilots, attempting this nerve-wracking stunt would "chicken out" at the last moment and bank sharply as they roared through the "fat man's squeeze"!

On very windy days at Drem, "Batty" would take off in a Tiger Moth, a small bi-plane trainer. Even if the wind speed was only a little faster than the stalling speed of the Tiger Moth, he would head the plane into the wind and then throttle back until the plane would start to slowly drift backwards! Sometimes it would stall and plunge downward. But at the last moment, having gained speed, he would pull out of the dive. He would do this several times, as we stood and watched in amazement at his breathtaking stunt.

I spent those very cold winter months at Drem on guard duty, either at the main gate or at a heavily wooded area on the south side of the airfield. A paved, U-shaped road ran through the woods with Hurricane fighters dispersed along either side under the large trees. It was perfect camouflage from enemy aircraft.

# SHOT DOWN!

We didn't look forward to our twenty-four-hour stint of guard duty at this wooded area since we had to sleep in a tent pitched on the frozen, snow-covered ground. Once I found a pheasant in the woods, caught in a poacher's trap. I boxed it up and mailed it to my married sister, Meriel, who lived near London.

On January 8, 1941, I joyfully boarded a train at the Drem railway station and headed south on my first seven-day leave. I had so much to tell my parents, and southern England was a welcome break from the frigid cold of Scotland. But the seven days passed all too soon, and it was time to return to guarding the Hurricane fighters at Drem.

About three weeks after I returned to base, a new posting came through for me, but again I experienced frustration as I was sent to Newcastle-on-Tyne in England for further guard duty. Would my observer training never start?

Finally one morning six weeks later, as I scanned the Daily Routine Orders (it was our responsibility to read these), I saw my name followed by instructions to report to the Duty Officer. I hurried to the DO's office.

The sergeant greeted me with a smile. "Your posting to Initial Training Wing (ITW) has come through. You're going to Torquay in Devon. Lucky chap, it will be a lot warmer there! Here's your train voucher. You have to be there by midday tomorrow. Don't be late, and good luck."

"Whoopee!" I yelled, as I grabbed the voucher and ran to the barracks to pack my kitbag. If I left straight away, I would be able to spend the night at home instead of traveling through the night. After some hasty goodbyes and much back slapping, I was on my way to the railway station. I don't think anyone ever left his unit as quickly as I did that morning!

As the train headed south, I sat listening to the click of the wheels on the rails. They played sweet music to my ears, "Your waiting is over; your waiting is over!"

Arriving at London, I phoned my mother to tell her I would be home in an hour.

"What are you doing in London?" she asked.

"Posted to Torquay," I replied excitedly. "I'll tell you more when I get home."

The eight-week course at ITW sped by as we learned the basics of navigational wireless, meteorology, the Morse code, and Air Force Law. To help us become proficient at recognizing both enemy and Allied aircraft, there were photos and silhouettes of every aircraft, showing them flying at different angles, all over the walls and doors of our rooms. We spent hours studying them.

At the end of the course, we were promoted to the rank of "Leading Aircraftsman" with a very welcome increase in pay. The next stage of our training odyssey would take us overseas, so we were given a seven-day embarkation leave to begin June 8, 1941.

*On embarkation leave at Ickenham*

Because the airfields in the British Isles were needed primarily for operational activity against the enemy, the Commonwealth Plan was created whereby pilots and observers received their practical flying training either in North America or in South Africa and Southern Rhodesia. When I was put on the list to go to Canada, I was thrilled because my mother's brother and sister had immigrated to that country before I was born. Now I would be able to see them and my four cousins for the first time.

But more frustration! At the last moment, when we were actually lined up in three columns ready to march to the boat train, I and two other men were told to fall out. Apparently the unit had three men too many, and since each of us was the last man in our respective columns, we were the first ones cut.

*The ration cards for my two embarkation leaves.*

After two or three days, I was sent back to my ITW at Torquay, where I was told I would be attached to the next group—a group that was going to South Africa. This group would not complete its training and be ready to go to Africa for two weeks. So for about a week, I just wandered around with nothing to do. I became an embarrassment to the ITW, so to get me out of the way, they sent me home on leave until the course was finished. My disappointment in not going to Canada was sweetened by a second embarkation leave totaling fifteen days!

During this extended leave, I celebrated my eighteenth birthday on June 30, with my mother fussing over me as only a loving mother can do. When my leave was over and I departed to return to my unit, my father gave me a firm, lingering handshake.

# ADVENTURES IN FOREIGN CLIMES

I traveled to West Kirby, in Cheshire, to join my new group of about one hundred other RAF personnel. From there we traveled to Liverpool to join the troopship *Reno del Pacifica* scheduled to sail for South Africa.

Our troopship was not a very large liner and in peacetime carried only about three hundred passengers. But now, as a wartime troopship, she was fitted out with three-tiered bunks and was able to carry some two thousand military personnel.

The morning after we boarded, our ship slipped out of Liverpool harbor before dawn and, hugging the west coast of England, made her way northward to the broad estuary of the River Clyde in Scotland. There she joined a large convoy of other ships, mostly freighters, which was ready to sail with its escort of numerous naval warships.

The speed of the convoy was governed by the speed of the slowest ship, and the trip to South Africa lasted a long seven weeks. To lessen the danger from prowling German U-boats and pocket battleships, the convoy sailed westward across the Atlantic Ocean until it almost reached Newfoundland. Then it headed south, sailing just out of sight of the North and South American continents. From time to time one or more ships would leave the convoy and head westward to some American port.

The monotony of this long, tedious journey was broken only once when the convoy sailed back across the mid-Atlantic for refueling at Freetown, Sierra Leone, on the west coast of Africa. In Freetown harbor I lost a silver cigarette case which my sister Barbara had given me just before I left England. I was leaning against the ship's railing, watching the native swimmers diving for the coins we were throwing to them, when the rail pushed the case out of my shirt pocket. It fell into the water and sank out of sight. An expensive loss!

Leaving Freetown, the ships remaining in the convoy steamed back toward South America before turning south. We continued in this southerly direction until we reached the latitude of the Cape of Good Hope at the southern tip of Africa. The convoy then headed back east toward Cape Town. By that time we felt we had seen all the water we ever wanted to!

One bright, sunny afternoon, while some of us were sunbathing on the foredeck of the ship, one of the men shouted excitedly, "Look, look!" Jumping up, we gazed in the direction he was pointing. Rising above the horizon, was a flat-topped mountain. We could hardly contain our excitement; it was the famous Table Mountain which dominates Cape Town. How the ancient mariners, after spending many long weeks in their slow sailing ships, must have thrilled when they saw that isolated mountain rising majestically above the eastern horizon! Soon the pitching and rolling of the ship, sometimes mild, sometimes severe, would be but a bad memory as we again stood on *terra firma,* good old Mother Earth.

In spite of all the excitement as the *Reno del Pacifica* tied up at the dock, I was once again to experience disappointment. We had all anticipated at least two thrilling days of shore leave after such a long voyage, but RAF Transportation had other plans. That same day, in what we considered unseemly haste, our contingent was herded onto a train for a tiring twenty-four-hour journey that took us overnight across the very cold Great Karroo Desert, and the next day through the sparsely populated expanse of the vast South African veldt. It was almost a thousand miles from Cape Town to the RAF staging camp between Johannesburg and Pretoria.

At last we were given a ten-day disembarkation leave. I had hooked up with Maurice Hapgood, another trainee observer. We all called him "Happy." He and I decided to spend our leave together in Durban, a very picturesque and interesting coastal city by the Indian Ocean.

Arriving at Durban we went straight to the servicemen's canteen, where we met Mrs. Jean Bolton, a volunteer. She kindly invited us to stay with her family while we were in Durban. The family showed us many of the interesting sights in and around the city, and we greatly enjoyed Mrs. B's fabulous cooking. The Boltons were a precious family, and Happy Hapgood and I came to love them. Mrs. Bolton kept in touch with us after we left.

Later I learned of the great sadness that came to this dear family. Jill, their lovely little daughter, became ill with infantile paralysis. In 1943, when I was a prisoner of war in Germany, Mrs. Bolton wrote to my mother saying, "Jill is very brave and of high courage. Control of her head, neck, and body muscles has returned, but her legs are still encased." Later she wrote, "Jill is continuing to make slow but sure progress, and some leg muscles are responding to treatment." She went on to say that they were building a swimming pool in their garden, since water exercise could play a major part in her full recovery. Prayers were being answered.

In wartime England we hadn't seen bananas for three years, and milk was strictly rationed. So one of our favorite afternoon pastimes while in Durban was to buy a dozen bananas and take them to a milk bar where we would wash them down with milkshakes.

Before leaving Durban I made sure I took a ride in a rickshaw pulled by a tall, majestic Zulu dressed in the fascinating splendor of his native costume with its colorful feathered head dress.

About a week after our leave, Hapgood and I, along with eleven other men, were posted to RAF 5 Squadron, 42 Air School, at Port Elizabeth on the southern coast to begin our observer training.

As an observer I was to be trained not only as a navigator, but also as a bomb aimer and an air gunner. After two weeks of class work, we began our flight training with gunnery practice, using a single-engine Fairy Battle plane. I will never forget the exhilarating thrill of becoming airborne for the very first time, seeing the ground drop away below me as the plane climbed into the sky like a bird.

Alongside, to starboard, another Fairy Battle was pulling a drogue—a long, tapered, open-ended cloth sleeve, like a windsock. This was my target. Standing in the open rear cockpit, the slipstream tugging at my flying jacket and helmet, I would take aim at the drogue and squeeze the trigger of the free-mounted machine gun, giving short bursts of fire. The accuracy of my aim would be determined by the number of bullet holes in the drogue—if any!

It was during this time that we heard about the bombing of Pearl Harbor and that the war had now widened to embrace the United States of America and Japan. Truly we were now engaged in a "world" war.

After air gunnery, the bomb-aiming course began. For the practical flight training the Fairy Battle was again used, but this time the experience was not so pleasant. When dropping smoke bombs on the rocky coastal range, I had to lie in the belly of the plane with the exhaust fumes of the engine (which was just in front of me) seeping into the area where I was lying. That was the only time I ever felt airsick.

It was most gratifying to see a grey puff of smoke rise from the target marked in white on the rocks below, indicating a direct hit. More often than not my puffs were wide of the target. I don't think I would have made a very good bomb aimer.

*Receiving my coveted Observer's wings. At last I am an Observer!*

Finally the time came when all our attention was given to navigation, which was the primary part of the observer course. Here was where my interest really lay, and I gave my complete, unreserved attention to the instructors during the many hours of lectures, learning dead-reckoning navigation, astronomical navigation, meteorology, and numerous other related subjects.

For the practical flight exercises we used a twin-engine Avro Anson; a pilot would fly the plane with two trainees aboard. Except for one big disadvantage, the Anson was a big step up from the Fairy Battle—this aircraft did not have a hydraulically operated undercarriage, which meant that once the plane was airborne one of the trainees had to crank a handle about one hundred and fifty turns to get the wheels up. By the time the wheels were fully retracted our arms would be aching. Upon landing, there was no problem; gravity took all the hard work out of lowering the undercarriage!

Throughout the twenty-week observer course, we were kept busy attending countless lectures, besides logging many hours of flying. Once we had successfully passed our exams, it was time for graduation when we would receive our coveted Observer's wings and be promoted to the rank of sergeant. What a high day of celebrating and back slapping!

The RAF wasted no time in sending us back to England, but before leaving Port Elizabeth, Happy and I made a last visit to our two "aunties" to say goodbye. Shortly after our arrival at Port Elizabeth we had met these two middle-aged sisters, Agnes and Mary Lake, at the servicemen's canteen. They had taken us under their wings, giving us a home away from home. They were delightful spinsters who had lost their fiancés in World War I when a South African regiment was almost totally wiped out in the terrible trench warfare in France. With such a relatively small number of persons of British descent in South Africa, the loss of a large group of young men caused many young women to remain widows or spinsters.

Our "aunties" took us on numerous picnics; one of our favorite spots was a grove of trees close to the Indian Ocean. Occasionally they took us out to their brother's farm where we went horseback riding. Once we were on a trail, riding through some scrub. For some reason I had dropped behind the rest of the party which was now out of sight. As I was cantering to catch up, my horse suddenly dug its hooves into the ground and stopped abruptly. I went sailing over its head. The horse then galloped off down the trail, round a bend, and out of sight. Sprinting after him, I rounded the bend and saw the rest of the party—with my horse. Mr. Lake, the farmer, thought the horse might have been frightened by a snake. I was none the worse for my spill.

While at the farm I tried my hand at milking a cow. I don't remember having had much success!

## SHOT DOWN!

*Able Seaman Just Nuisance with some of his sailor friends*

*The statue of this famous Great Dane in Jubilee Square, Simon's Town, South Africa*

A few days after saying goodbye to our "aunties," we began the long train journey to Cape Town, along with the other men in our group. The train took us on a very scenic route as it wound between the mountains that rose toward the sky on our right and the Indian Ocean stretching away to the horizon on our left.

In Cape Town, we had a few days for sightseeing before embarking on the *Empress of Japan* for our voyage back to England. Hapgood and I took the opportunity to go to the top of Table Mountain, so called because of its flat top and the fact that it was often draped with a cloud giving the appearance of a tablecloth. We made the ascent by the cable car as we didn't have enough time to make the challenging climb on foot.

A fond memory I have of Cape Town is meeting one of its most celebrated citizens—Able Seaman Just Nuisance. When I met him in the Union Jack Club, a canteen for servicemen in Cape Town, he was the sole occupant of a large couch, lying with his four legs sticking straight up in the air. Yes, that's right, *four* legs. You see, he was a Great Dane! One of the amazing things about Just Nuisance was that he actually held the rank of Able Seaman in the British Navy, and his name, rank, and number were recorded at Admiralty House in London. I had read about this famous dog in a book. Whenever Just Nuisance saw sailors on the streets of Cape Town, he seemed to know when one of them had had too much to drink, and would gently take the inebriated sailor by the sleeve of his jacket and lead him to the railway station. A railway official would then put the sailor on a train going to Simons Town where the naval base was located. It was said that Just Nuisance knew the time of the last train in the evening and never missed it! Another amazing thing about this animal was that he seemed to be able to count. At least he could tell the difference between Sunday, when the last train left one hour earlier, and the other six days of the week. Because of the service he rendered to the sailors, he also had a bunk at the naval base. And no one dared disturb him when he occupied one of the few couches in the canteen!

We embarked, all too soon, on the *Empress of Japan,* a large liner that had just arrived from the Far East with 450 women and children, refugees from Singapore, which had fallen to the Japanese. Also on board were about 150 merchant seamen whose ships had been torpedoed. Including our RAF contingent of 45, there were only about 650 passengers. Since the *Empress of Japan* had not yet been converted into a troopship, there were plenty of comfortable peacetime accommodations. (Shortly after her arrival in England the *Empress of Japan* was renamed the *Empress of Canada.*)

Being a fast ship, the *Empress* sailed without naval escort, depending on her speed to outrun any lurking enemy U-boats. She made the voyage to Liverpool in the pre-war time of fifteen days. We saw no sign of the enemy during the voyage to England, but the repeated changing of course and the presence of those 150 sailors whose ships had been sunk, constantly reminded us of the dangers lurking in the ocean. And though there was a general lightheartedness, with dancing most evenings, one could sense it was just a façade, hiding the tension everyone felt. A question on many minds was: "Had the authorities made the right decision in sending us home without a naval escort?"

As the ship skirted the Bay of Biscay, drawing nearer to the highly dangerous waters surrounding the British Isles, the tension among the passengers rose markedly. Only on March 27, 1942, when we steamed into Liverpool harbor and tied up at the dock, did they show their profound relief. Some reacted with lighthearted banter and back slapping. But many of the women broke down and wept, some sobbing uncontrollably. The trauma they had so recently experienced and not knowing the fate of their husbands was too much for them.

# MY TRAINING ENDS

For a lad not yet nineteen years old, the past eight-and-a-half months had been a never-to-be-forgotten adventure that had taken me to far-off exotic places. But now I was happy to be back in England and nearer to my goal—the squadron and revenge!

First, however, came our fourteen-day disembarkation leave and the excitement of seeing my parents and two sisters again. I told them about the places I had seen and all the things I had done and learned. The days passed quickly and enjoyably, until one evening the wailing of the air-raid sirens reminded me that England was in the front line of a bitter war. It was time to move on.

Once again bidding my parents goodbye, I traveled to the RAF station at Millom, Cumberland, for a six-week course in advanced navigation. Here I honed my navigational skills, getting accustomed to the widely varying weather conditions of England which I had not experienced in the balmy clime of South Africa.

One warm, sunny day I found myself drawn to the lakes and rolling hills which lay to the north of Millom. This area is one of England's most renowned beauty spots—the Lake District. We had the day off, so three friends and I decided to spend the afternoon hiking among these hills. Let me quote from a letter I wrote to my parents on May 25, 1942:

> We caught a train to Coniston and started hiking from there. I have never seen such beauty before anywhere. We

walked to a lake called Tarn Hawes. There was nothing except an old fence to show that anybody had ever been there before, it was so wild. We climbed up Hawkshead Hill, and from it we could see four lakes sprawled around at the bottom. On one side was Lake Windermere, then turning to 3 o'clock was Esthwait Water, then to 6 o'clock Lake Coniston, and lastly to 9 o'clock Tarn Hawes Water. It was a stupendous view!

The quiet serenity of this oasis of nature's beauty completely embraced me, removing all thought of the war that was raging in much of the world.

As the afternoon wore on we began to feel hungry, so we decided it was time to head back to Coniston. Along a narrow country lane we came across a small farmhouse where a prominent sign invited "Farm House Teas." "Wow, we're in luck!" one of my friends exclaimed as, without breaking step, we turned in at the gate.

The farmer's friendly wife greeted us with a warm smile and led us into a charmingly decorated parlor where a table was already laid. And what a fantastic English tea it was! Except for the tea we drank, everything was home produced and homemade. For only eighteen pence (twenty-one U.S. cents) we tucked into a fresh boiled egg, plenty of bread, butter, strawberry jam, scones, and delicious fruit cake. With the strict food rationing necessary in England, we hadn't seen food like that since before the war.

We continued hiking in the cool of the evening before heading back to camp. We all agreed we had spent a memorable day away from our preparations for war.

Later that week, I went on a training flight that took us out over the Irish Sea to the southwestern end of the Caledonian Canal, then along the canal to Inverness at the canal's North Sea end. This unique waterway consists of several connected lochs and divides Scotland in two. One of these natural lakes is the famous Loch Ness. Did we hope to see the monster as we flew over? Landing at the Inverness RAF airfield, we enjoyed a couple of hours of relaxation before heading back to base.

On the homeward trip our pilot was mischievous. Seeing a fisherman in his small boat on one of the lochs, he dove down almost to water level and headed straight for the boat. The fisherman dropped his fishing pole and fell flat in his boat! We roared with laughter, but I'm sure the poor man didn't find this unkind act at all funny.

Another of my memories of Millom involves a training flight and a tooth. Shortly after having a tooth filled I went on a training flight. As the plane started to climb, my tooth began to ache. The higher we went, the more it hurt, until the pain became so excruciating I could no longer concentrate on my navigation. Only when we lost height did the terrible pain subside. When I went back to the dentist and described what had happened, he told me that a small pocket of air must have been trapped under the filling. He refilled the tooth, and thankfully I had no further trouble.

With the completion of the advanced navigational course, the end of our long observer training was now in sight. It seemed such a long time since I had started my aircrew training at the Initial Training Wing. With a growing sense of purpose and urgency, I left Millom for the Operational Training Unit (OTU) at Lichfield in Staffordshire. The OTU would be our final phase of training before being posted to the squadron. Now I began to feel a little of the apprehension that was part of operational aircrew life. Oh, I would still laugh, but maybe not quite so readily.

Arriving at Lichfield, I reported to the administration office and learned that I would be part of Course 21. Each course was made up of an equal number of pilots, navigators, bomb aimers, wireless operators, and air gunners—about seventy men. The individual crews were not formed arbitrarily by assigning men to a particular group. Instead, we formed our own crews based on the friendships we developed over the first week or so of this final training. This led to strong bonds between the men of each crew; we trusted each other and had complete confidence in our crew mates.

After getting settled in the barracks assigned to me, I wandered over to the sergeants' mess. Almost immediately I heard someone call, "Hey, Curnow!" Turning, I was delighted to see John Todd, "Toddy" we called him. I had last seen Toddy when we disembarked from the *Empress of Japan*. He had trained with me in South Africa.

After a warm handshake, Toddy asked, "Have you crewed up yet?"

"Not yet," I replied, "I've only just arrived."

"I haven't crewed up yet, either," he said. "Are you a navigator or a bomb aimer?" (Observers functioned as either navigators or bomb aimers.)

"A navigator."

"I'm a bomb aimer. How about us crewing up together?"

"Perfect," I replied. I had always liked Toddy; he was a quiet, dependable fellow, quite a bit older than I. He was in his early thirties.

"Great. By the way, I've already met a pilot who is looking for a navigator and a bomb aimer. He seems like a really nice fellow. Let me go find him." And with that, he hurried off.

Later in the afternoon Toddy found me again. "John, come and meet the pilot I told you about and see what you think. He already has a wireless operator and a rear gunner, and they are together right now."

As soon as I saw John Roper I knew I wanted him as my pilot. He appeared somewhat tense, but self-controlled at the same time. And there was something about him that bred confidence. I also took an immediate liking to the other two men—John Dobie, the wireless operator, and Ernest Waghorn, the rear gunner.

The big question was: Would Roper want a teenager as his navigator? The other navigators in our course were all more mature men in their midtwenties to midthirties. After introductions

*The original crew. Left to right: Ernest Waghorn, John Roper, John Todd. Front: John Dobie. Inset: John Curnow.*

and handshakes, we sat down and told each other about ourselves. Before long, we unanimously agreed to crew up together, which made us one of the first crews to be formed.

We laughed a little because four of us were named John, and we ribbed Waghorn for not being named John also. How would we handle this rather unique situation? We decided that John Roper would be either "Johnny" or "Skipper." John Todd would be "Toddy," John Dobie would be "Jock" since he was a Scotsman, and I would be "John" or "Nav." And, of course, it was a forgone conclusion that Waghorn would be known as "Waggy." From then on we spent as much time together as possible so that we would really get to know one another.

During the first two weeks of the training, the pilots practiced circuits and bumps (takeoffs and landings) so as to become thoroughly

familiar with the Wellington bomber we would be using. For the rest of the crews, however, time dragged as we attended hours of boring lectures! Finally Roper was ready for us to move to the satellite airfield at Tatenhill,

*A Vickers-Armstrong Wellington bomber*

where we began six weeks of intensive flying together as a crew. During this time we became welded into a cohesive unit, ready for the rigors of operational flying.

The Wellington was a highly regarded, rugged, twin-engine bomber that had been the backbone of Bomber Command in the earlier years of the war. The "Wimpie," as it was affectionately called, required a crew of five.

On June 30, a few days after moving to Tatenhill, I celebrated my nineteenth birthday, though the crew and everyone else believed it was my twentieth. I never let on that I had put my age up when I enlisted.

# MY TRAINING ENDS

About this time I began to sense that the atmosphere at OTU was different from the previous training units I had experienced. At first, I wasn't able to put my finger on just what it was that was different, but gradually I realized that there wasn't the same sense of light-heartedness that I had generally found during the earlier stages of training. Instead, I detected a greater degree of seriousness that often showed on the faces of the men. Being aircrew and sporting wings on our jackets no longer seemed quite so glamorous. After all, we were now only weeks away from flying into enemy territory where death was ever present, both on the ground below and in the skies above.

After a few weeks, we started night flying for the first time. It was on one of these night exercises that our crew nearly came unglued! This particular night we were routed to Skegness on the east coast, then southwest to Oxford, and finally back north to Tatenhill. At the navigators' briefing the officer said, "Navigators, you'll need to pay very careful attention to this spot on the final leg," and he pointed to an area on the large map of England on the wall. "You see how we are routing you quite close to the city of Rugby which has a balloon barrage.[1] Take note, you will not be flying at an altitude higher than those balloons! So mark this spot on your charts and be careful not to be off course!" I dutifully marked Rugby on my navigational chart before leaving the briefing room.

During the exercise, all was going well as we reached our turning point near Oxford and headed north on the final leg. After a while I was able to get a fix that showed the wind had changed a little and that we were about five miles off course to the east. Though we were nearing Rugby with its balloon barrage, I judged from my chart that we would pass some five miles west of the city, so I was not concerned. I began to calculate the correction needed to get back on track.

A few minutes later Waggy, the rear gunner, said over the intercom, "Navigator, we've just passed over a sausage-shaped lake."

I was consulting my topographical map when Toddy, who was sitting in the front gun turret, said, "There's another lake like that ahead." Then a second later he yelled, "No, it's a balloon!"

I was thrown backward as Roper banked violently to port to avoid crashing into the huge silvery mass that suddenly loomed before us. Flying on its wingtip, the Wellington almost scraped the barrage balloon as we thundered past. With his eyes peeled and with timely warnings from Toddy, Roper was able to skillfully maneuver the plane out of this lethal hazard.

I was staring in bewilderment at my navigational chart, wondering what could have gone wrong, when Roper's grim voice came over the intercom, "What kind of a navigator have I got? If we get back alive, I'm going to get myself a new one!"

The rest of the flight was completed in silence except for a few navigational instructions I had to give Roper to guide the plane back to Tatenhill airfield.

After landing, with a very shaken-up crew, for we had come within feet of being killed, I went to the briefing room to find out what mistake I had made. I quickly found out. I had marked Rugby on my chart one longitudinal line to the east of where I should have marked it. This meant that instead of being five miles to the east, as my chart had shown, Rugby had been dead ahead. I never made that kind of mistake again.

But was I now without a crew? Would Johnny Roper carry out his threat? Nervously I explained to him the mistake I had made. He responded, "OK, but be more careful in the future." And with that nothing further was said.

At nineteen I was the kid of the crew. Toddy, the oldest, was thirty-two, married, and had two children. Then came Waggy, who was twenty-seven and single. Next was Jock, twenty-five and married, but without any children. Finally, there was Johnny, our skipper, who was twenty-two and married, but also with no children. I considered myself very fortunate to be allowed to remain the navigator of such a steady and decent crew.

Not long after this incident, Johnny Roper and I went for a stroll into the nearby countryside. A mile or so from the airfield, we met a farmer and stopped for a chat. We talked about the war for a while before the conversation turned to farming and its vital contribution to the war effort. Of course, food rationing came up, and when we mentioned how small our egg ration was, the farmer offered to sell us some eggs if we wanted them. We jumped at this opportunity to augment our egg ration. Since I had a bicycle, many were the times I cycled to this farm and came back with two or three dozen eggs.

We made a deal with the cook at the sergeants' mess—he would fix a couple of eggs on toast for each of us, while he kept two eggs for himself. Everyone was happy with this deal!

In one of my letters to my parents I wrote:

> I've found a farm not far from the 'drome[2] where I can buy as many eggs as I want. And, oh boy, what breakfasts we have!
>
> Do you know that my crew gets through seventy eggs a week? We each have two eggs in the morning and sometimes extra ones at tea time.

Soon the time came when we were ready to move on to a squadron. We were given a few days leave, with instructions to report to Royal Air Force 103rd Squadron at Elsham Wolds in North Lincolnshire.

This was it! No more larking about and frivolous joviality. Now, twenty three months after looking at that hand on the poster in the train, pointing straight at me with the words YOUR COUNTRY NEEDS YOU, I was finally to arrive at the squadron. After nearly eighteen months of training, I believed I was well prepared for the deadly business of frontline warfare, for life or death.

---

[1] A balloon barrage is a screen of large tethered balloons flown over a city or other area to protect it from low flying enemy aircraft.

[2] Our shorthand for "aerodrome" which, in turn, is "British" for "airfield."

# PAYBACK TIME

I spent a peaceful few days in Ickenham with my parents, enjoying the unusually warm summer sunshine while working in their attractive English flower garden. But, as my leave drew to an end, I started to hear within me the drumbeats of war. I remembered how the night sky over my beloved London had turned red as fires raged below and German bombs blasted whole blocks into rubble and hundreds of innocent men, women, and children into eternity! It was payback time now, time for me to give back to the Nazis some of the horror they had brought to London, Coventry, Amsterdam, Rotterdam, Warsaw, and many other European cities. At that time, God had little or no place in my young heart; there was room there only for a spirit of revenge!

But I also remembered how many German airmen had perished in the skies over England as their planes were shot down. So it was not without a little apprehension that I said Goodbye to my mother and father. They held me in tight embraces, as if not wanting to let me go, for they recognized better than I did the mortal dangers into which I was headed. Hadn't my father fought on the bloodstained battlefields of France only twenty-four years earlier against the same enemy?

Shouldering my kitbag, I headed down the road to catch the bus that would take me to the local railway station. I looked back and gave a final goodbye wave. As I did so the thought flashed through my mind: *Will I ever see them again?*

# PAYBACK TIME

Arriving at Barnetby Junction, the nearest railway station to Elsham Wolds, in the late afternoon, I was thankful the extremely hot train journey was over. In my first letter home from Elsham Wolds, sent on August 28, 1942, I wrote:

> Oh what a journey! I was cooked. The train I traveled up in was frightful; absolutely no ventilation at all, and I boiled. To show how hot it was, I was unable to eat any of the food until I changed at Retford. The sandwiches proved very useful and also very tasty as I didn't get to the camp until six o'clock in the evening.

My mother kept all my letters, so I am able to quote from them today. Also the August 27 entry in my squadron's old Operation Record Book states, "Heat wave sets in after very unsettled and unseasonable spell." And on the 28th it stated, "Heat wave reached peak with a ground temperature of 86 degrees." I was happy, therefore, to see RAF transport waiting at the station to take any personnel to the aerodrome. To have walked two and a half miles uphill in that heat would have been grim!

I had strong, but mixed, emotions as the guard at the gate waved the personnel-carrier through and we made our way to the administration building. My heart beat faster as I saw some huge bombers parked in the distance, and I felt great satisfaction that I was, at last, attached to a bomber command squadron. But my elation was tempered by the realization that all this led to one purpose—war! The date I arrived at the bomber squadron, August 26, 1942, is forever engraved in my memory.

Checking in at the orderly room I was given temporary quarters for the night and told to report back the next day. In his excellent book, *An Erk's Eye View of World War II,* Ted Mawdsley describes the orderly room as being "the nerve centre of all administration and the source of all the countless and myriad forms on which the RAF depended for its very existence." By late evening the rest of the crew had arrived. The next morning we met at the orderly room, at which time we were assigned to our permanent quarters. With Skipper

Johnny Roper leading the way, we reported as a crew to the squadron office and were welcomed by the commanding officer, Wing Commander[1] R. A. C. Carter. We also met Squadron Leaders[2] C. K. Saxelby and Sidney Fox, the two flight commanders.

The 103rd Squadron was equipped with four-engine Halifax heavy bombers, so we had to go through a three-week conversion program. This was especially important for the pilot and the flight engineer. The flight engineer was one of two new crew members we had to acquire, the other being an additional gunner to man the mid-upper gun turret. Since the Halifax was a much larger bomber than the Wellington, it required a crew of seven.

We could hardly believe it when we learned the name of the flight engineer assigned to our crew—John Rose. We now had five Johns in the crew! It was only natural that we give him the nickname, "Rosie." At least our new mid-upper gunner—Charles Duncan— was not named John!

That first letter I wrote home from the squadron continued:

> My first impressions of this camp aren't much. Though what I can say for it is the food is very good and so are the sleeping quarters; we have a large room between two of us, about the size of the middle bedroom [of our home]. It [Elsham Wolds] is the most outlandish spot I've been to. The nearest fair-sized town is Grimsby which is about half an hour's bus ride away. There are other smaller places much nearer, but the problem is that it is so hard to get to them from the 'drome.

As I got to know more people and became fully involved in the mission of the squadron, I got used to living on top of a "wold," which I learned means a fairly high, wind-swept area. And usually there was enough RAF transport to get around.

I was happy to find that my Raleigh sport bicycle had arrived safely from Lichfield. It would receive considerable use on this sprawling RAF station, with the dispersal points (where the bombers were parked) dotted all around the perimeter of the airfield.

## PAYBACK TIME

Though we were attached to the Conversion Flight and therefore not yet directly involved with the operational life of the squadron, we still felt the emotional impact of the losses the squadron was incurring. During the two nights following our arrival at Elsham Wolds, three bombers were lost on raids to Kassel, Saarbrucken, and Nuremberg. A week later two more aircraft failed to return, one of which was piloted by S/L Saxelby, the senior flight commander. This was a big shock to the squadron.

At the end of our conversion we were assigned to "A Flight." Finally we were officially part of an operational squadron! We had carried out numerous flying exercises during our conversion; now we, and the squadron, believed we were ready for operations against the enemy. When would that first combat mission come?

Right at this time poor weather conditions over Europe caused a lull in operations, and it wasn't until October 2 that the squadron resumed active missions with a raid on Krefeld. Our pilot, Roper, in order to get "blooded," went on that raid as the copilot of an experienced crew. All ten aircraft returned safely. Of course, I and the rest of our crew were full of questions when he returned. "What was it like, Skipper?" "Did you see any night fighters?" "How heavy was the flak?" We would have those questions answered soon enough in an awesomely dangerous way, but we would have to wait a little longer. The following day it was our turn on the roster to have our first six-day leave. Once on the squadron, aircrews received six days leave every six weeks, provided they survived long enough!

Arriving back in Ickenham, I quickly forgot about squadron life as I enjoyed the comfort of my own bed, late mornings, and my mother's cooking. Looking from my upstairs bedroom window I could see, at the end of our long garden, the thicket in which my sister Barbara and I had played as children. On the far side of the thicket was the small River Pin in which I had paddled and fished for minnows. Beyond, I could see familiar sites—the public land on which was a lake with two small islands, and in the distance, rising above some trees, the roof of the old Swakelays Manor House built in 1629. According to local legend, a tunnel had once connected the manor house to the old St. Giles church. This church, with its

*Swakeleys Manor House in old Ickenham*

medieval bell, was built in the late fourteenth century. It seemed a lifetime ago since those peaceful pre-war days when lazy games of cricket were played on the manicured grass in front of the old manor.

Quickly it was time to say goodbye to my parents. I needed to leave home in the morning in order to arrive at the squadron before midnight, but my father had left for work before I had awakened, so I waited until he came home. Because of this I didn't arrive back at the squadron until early the next morning. I was nabbed at the main gate, and my late arrival was reported to the squadron office.

When I arrived at the room I shared with Johnny Roper, he remonstrated with me for returning late. He then told me it had been a bad week while we had been on leave. On October 5 ten kites (our slang for an airplane) had gone to Aachen, and one of the senior crews, piloted by Warrant Officer K. F. Edwards, had failed to return. Then the following night, on a raid to Osnabruck, Sergeant J. Porter and crew were lost on their fourth mission. With seven crews lost in six operations, a somber mood had settled over the squadron.

On the afternoon of October 13 we were relaxing in the lounge of the sergeants' mess when the squadron duty sergeant announced over the loudspeaker: "Attention all aircrews! Attention all aircrews! There will be operations tonight. Pilots and navigators will report to the navigation briefing room at 1500 hours. Main briefing will be at 1700 hours."

Pin-drop silence momentarily fell in the mess. I felt a rush of adrenalin and started to breathe heavily. "Get a grip on yourself, Curnow," I said to myself. "This is what you wanted and what you have trained for." Conversation started to pick up again, but voices were noticeably subdued. Some tried to pretend that it was no big deal, but no one was fooled.

About half an hour later Roper found me and said, "Time to go, Nav." We left the mess and made our way to the navigation briefing room, along with eleven other navigators and their pilots. Glancing up into the almost cloudless sky, Roper observed pensively, "Not much cloud cover tonight." Clouds were the night-flying bombers' friends!

In the briefing room stood some twenty draftsman-type tables; for maximum security, the room was windowless. Selecting a vacant table, I spread out my navigational chart, ready to work out my flight plan. The table I had selected would remain mine for the next five months, and through those months I would see a heavy turnover of navigators as plane after plane failed to return from a mission. In fact, by the end of January 1943, only one other navigator who was in the room that October 13 evening, would still be there with me— Sgt. A. F. Reif, a Canadian belonging to Bunny Austin's crew.

That evening when everyone had gathered, the senior squadron navigation officer announced, "Tonight, gentlemen, the target is Kiel, and this will be your route." Turning to the large topographical map of Europe on the wall, he wound a strand of red wool around several pins in the map to outline the route. The plan was for about three hundred and fifty bombers from some twenty-five to twenty-seven squadrons, to converge over Skegness, a town on the east coast of England. From there we would fly in a stream over the North Sea, crossing the Danish peninsula about twenty miles south of Kiel, and then turn north to the target.

The navigation officer gave us the anticipated speed and direction of the wind and the exact longitude and latitude of the turning points. He also gave us the height and speed at which we were to fly and the estimated time of arrival (ETA) at the target.

"Any questions, gentlemen?" he asked. "OK, if there are no questions, start working on your flight plans."

We were handed packets of top secret information containing the current wireless frequencies and codes of the flashing beacons which were dotted all over the country. This information was printed on rice paper which could be quickly destroyed by swallowing.

At this point Roper and the other pilots left to check that their planes were ready for the operation. They would also make sure that the other members of the crews were checking that their guns, wireless equipment, and bombsights were in perfect working order.

Since this was my first operation I was a little nervous. I wanted to be absolutely sure I was doing things correctly. So I checked once or twice with some veteran navigators who assured me I was doing OK.

It was the duty of the last navigator leaving the room to remove from the wall map all evidence of the target. Because I had been a bit slow working out my flight plan this first time, this responsibility fell to me. Security had to be maintained at a high level, even on a tightly guarded air force base. In fact, prior to the main briefing, only the pilots and navigators knew what the target would be. The fewer persons who had early knowledge of the actual target, the better it would be for security. Also the telephones were locked down so that no thoughtless individual could say anything about the operation while phoning someone.

After an early meal, all eighty-four crew members of the twelve bombers trooped into the large main briefing room, which was also windowless. Soon it was filled with tobacco smoke. As we sat waiting, small groups talked among themselves, but any light-heartedness was a mask for the underlying tension we were all experiencing.

Punctually at 1700 hours Wing Commander Carter walked into the room with the senior intelligence officer, the meteorological officer, and the two flight commanders. S/L J. H. Kennard was the new flight commander, taking the place of S/L Saxelby. As the officers entered, silence fell, and we all sprang to attention.

"At ease, gentlemen," W/C Carter said, and we all sat down, giving him our full attention.

"The weather is good, so operations will definitely be on tonight," he said in his crisp, precise manner. I heard one or two heavy sighs nearby. "Please give careful attention to the intelligence and weather reports."

Stepping to the wall facing us, S/L Shepperd, the senior intelligence officer, pulled aside the black curtain covering a very large topographical map of Europe. Pointing to a large red spot marking the target area, he said, "Gentlemen, your target tonight is Kiel. In a few minutes we will show close-up photos of the city and the dock area with its submarine pens. These pens will be your aiming point, and it is important that we destroy them, so bomb aimers, when you pick up your copies of the close-ups after the briefing, be sure to study them well and memorize the important landmarks. We want accurate bombing tonight!"

Pointing to the route, which was marked with a red thread, S/L Shepperd continued, "You will notice we are routing you quite close to Heligoland. Not all of you are familiar with this extremely dangerous island. It bristles with searchlights and flak guns, so navigators, be sure you keep your kites on track! One more thing before we look at the close-ups, this whole area swarms with night fighters, so all of you, especially the gunners, keep a sharp lookout for them."

The lights were then dimmed as the close-ups were flashed on the screen. The officer pointed out those landmarks which would be important for the bomb aimers to recognize.

By this time we smokers were drawing deeply on our cigarettes, and the meteorological officer's weather report didn't help to untie the knots in our stomachs. Pointing to the weather chart on the screen, he said, "Gentlemen, the weather conditions over the target should be excellent for bombing, with little or no cloud to hinder your visibility of the target."

"Yeah," came the voice of one of the airmen, "excellent for Jerry night fighters, too!" This was followed by some nervous laughter.

The group fell silent again as the lights came back on and S/L Fox, now the senior flight commander, spoke to us for a few minutes. He refocused our attention on the mission before us, which was to disrupt and hamper the U-boat menace which was threatening the very lifelines of our country. In so doing he took our minds off the personal fears that all aircrews experienced to some degree as they faced the mortal dangers lurking in the enemy skies. As the future station commander, Group Captain[3] L. W. Dickens would later say, "If any airman says he is not afraid, he is either a fool or a liar." How very true! He made this comment to Don Charlwood, a senior navigator, when interviewing him for his commission.

After Fox had finished his short but very timely pep talk, the squadron commander, or "wingco," again spoke about the strategic importance of the target, reminding the bomb aimers to study the photos carefully for accurate bombing. Pausing, he slowly looked over us all with his piercing eyes, nodded his head ever so slightly, and said, "Good luck, gentlemen." He well knew he might not see some of us again.

The briefing was over, and we made our way to the operations room where we had our individual lockers and equipment. It was now time for us to get all our gear together for the flight. Being the navigator I was loaded down more than the other members of my crew. Besides my parachute, I had to lug with me the automatic astronomical sextant and my heavy navigator's bag bulging with the navigational chart, numerous topographical maps, other navigational equipment, and a thermos flask filled with steaming hot coffee.

The last thing we did before leaving the operations room for the dispersal point, where our fully loaded bomber awaited us, was to buckle on our parachute harnesses and stuff an escape kit into a pocket. This escape kit contained some French and German money, three silk maps covering the European continent, water purification tablets, a small, button-sized compass, a six-inch hacksaw blade, and a small packet of concentrated food. It was intended for use in the event of being shot down and surviving. I think it gave us a psychological boost as we were comforted with the thought that we had a chance of surviving if we were shot down.

Finally it was time to climb into the trucks that were waiting to take the crews to the planes. Each truck carried two crews, so we climbed aboard ours with another crew.

"This is your first op, isn't it?" a member of the other crew asked.

"Yes, we're one of the two rookie crews."

"At least you'll be over the North Sea most of the time. Just steer clear of Heligoland and watch out for bandits,"[4] he said.

After a few minutes our truck pulled

*A Halifax bomber taking off at evening*

up at the dispersal point for "B-Bertie," which was our aircraft. We and the other crew wished each other good luck.

My thoughts were now fully occupied with the job at hand, as were those of each crew member. We all knew our survival depended upon each of us being on top of our individual jobs. There was now no time to dwell on the dangers ahead.

As we walked toward our plane, silhouetted menacingly against the early evening western sky, the members of our ground crew gave us the thumbs-up, wishing us good luck. One of them took my parachute and sextant, handing them up to me after I had climbed aboard. Moving forward, I stowed my parachute and sextant near my table, spread out my chart and made sure everything I needed was in place. I was now ready to enter the takeoff time on my log sheet.

Meanwhile Johnny Roper and Rosie, the engineer, had started the four engines and checked all the gauges, and the other crew members had made their last-minute checks. We were now ready to taxi to the runway. I went back to the doorway where the ground crew sergeant handed me the clearance certificate, which I gave to Roper to sign. I returned this to the sergeant who wished us good luck. Pulling up the ladder, I closed and fastened the door.

Roper now gave the thumbs-up signal to one of the ground crew who pulled away the wheel chocks. Slowly Roper taxied B-Bertie round the perimeter to the takeoff runway.

One by one, the bombers ahead of us roared down the runway until it was our turn. As Roper turned the Halifax onto the runway, I stood just behind Rosie in the cockpit area, the position I always took for takeoffs and landings. Roper slowly opened the throttles while still keeping the brakes on until the big plane was shaking and straining, ready to lunge forward as soon as the brakes were released. As the heavily laden bomber surged forward, gained speed, and finally lifted off, I experienced for the first time the special blend of exhilaration and apprehension that I would always feel when taking off on a bombing mission.

I glanced at my RAF navigator's watch which I had earlier adjusted to the second. The time which I entered on my log sheet was exactly 18.36 hours.[5]

Roper now put B-Bertie into the climbing pattern in which we circled the aerodrome, slowly gaining height to three or four thousand feet. I double-checked our course to Skegness and called Roper on the intercom, "Skipper, Navigator here. Our course for Skegness is 142 degrees. Please let me know when you set course and also our height and air speed. Our bombing height should be 10,000 feet. Over."

"Roger, Navigator."

"Navigator, Pilot here. Turning onto course. Height 3,500 and continuing to climb. Air speed 210. Over."

"Roger, Skipper. ETA Skegness in 15 minutes at 1904 hours."

"Roger, Navigator."

Before reaching our turning point I gave Roper the course which would take us over the North Sea, and at the correct time I instructed him to alter course.

Our course of about eighty degrees routed us some twenty miles north of Heligoland. By the time we were nearing the vicinity of this dangerous island it was quite dark, and I informed the crew that we had now entered enemy airspace.

Roper cut in, "Gunners, keep your eyes skinned for Jerry night fighters. Wireless op, you watch out through the astrodome, and

Engineer, you be on the lookout, too. Remember, most kites are lost through night fighters."

Roper now started flying a weaving pattern, which was down to port, then down to starboard, then up to port, followed by up to starboard. In this way, we flew with a corkscrew motion. He would continue flying this weaving pattern as long as we were in enemy airspace, except for the critical straight and level bombing run over the target.

About ten miles beyond Heligoland we altered course some thirteen degrees to starboard so as to cross the Danish peninsula fifteen miles south of Kiel. As we approached the coast, I asked Toddy, the bomb aimer, to check with his topographical map to see if he could get a pinpoint in the moonlight—a feature on the ground that could be identified on the map. One could often get a good location when crossing a coastline in moonlight. Luckily, because of the rugged nature of this coast, he was able to get a good pinpoint.

As we crossed the coast near the small German town of Heidi, Toddy announced over the intercom in somber tone, "Hey fellows, we are now flying over Germany for the first time." Nobody said anything.

"Skipper, Navigator here. We will reach the turning point for our run into the target in 15 minutes at 2129 hours. We are on track and on time."

Using Toddy's pinpoint, I was able to work out the actual velocity and direction of the wind we had been experiencing. I then calculated our course back to England, which I gave to Roper before we reached the target. That way he would be ready to head out once the bombs had been dropped. Even before we got to the turning point we could see the results of the bombing that had already started. I wouldn't need to give Roper a new course. All he had to do was to head toward the fires!

Now that navigation was out of my hands for a short while, I left my cabin and stood in the cockpit behind Rosie. As I looked at the inferno up ahead, my mind went back to the fires that burned night after night in London. I had no feelings of doubt or remorse about what we were going to do—only satisfaction that now it was payback time.

As we approached the city, which was vigorously fighting back, we saw scores of searchlights probing the night sky, seeking out the messengers of death in the darkness above. One could visualize the gunners below, tensely waiting for a bomber to be caught in the searchlights so they could open fire.

Suddenly Rosie shouted, "Searchlight to starboard!"

I saw a huge beam coming straight toward us. Knowing it would be impossible to avoid the searchlight, Roper unhesitatingly threw B-Bertie into a violent bank to starboard, taking the bomber straight into the oncoming beam. For an instant we were in the dazzling blue-white glare as we passed through the beam and into the darkness beyond before the German searchlight crew below could stop the swing of the light. We all breathed a sigh of relief and were thankful for Rosie's watchful eye and our pilot's brilliant maneuver. That was the only time in the six months we were on the squadron that we were caught in a searchlight.

Now it was time for Toddy, our bomb aimer, to take over.

"Hold it straight and level. Steady now, steady. A little to port. Steady. Bombs gone." The plane lurched upward as eight thousand pounds of high explosive and incendiary bombs dropped away.

"Hold it steady, Skipper, hold it steady. Photograph taken. Let's get out of this hell!" Toddy shouted as we all saw several searchlights moving in our direction.

Roper banked the lightened bomber hard to port, away from the searchlights, and with strong evasive action got B-Bertie clear of the target area.

"Keep your eyes skinned for Jerries," Roper said in a tense, but controlled, voice. "We're not out of it yet. This is when crews sometimes let down their guard, and Jerry fighters know it."

I went back to my table and noted in my log the time and height at which the bombs were dropped—2136 hours, at 10,000 feet.

"Skipper, Navigator here. We'll cross the coast in about 17 minutes, and we will be past Heligoland in half an hour. Our ETA at Elsham Wolds is 0057 hours."

"Roger, Navigator. Don't forget, everyone, the next half hour will be critical. Night fighters will be swarming!"

Once clear of the target area things were quiet, though we were still on the alert.

"Toddy to Navigator. Coast coming up. Do you want me to try to get another pinpoint? It's a bit cloudy now, though."

"Thanks a lot, Toddy, but I got a good wind from your pinpoint coming in, so you needn't bother. At least we won't have to worry anymore about flak," I replied.

"What about Heligoland?" Roper asked.

"We came off the target on track, so we will pass well clear of that place," I replied.

"We've still got to watch out for bandits."

"Hey, is that you, Waggy? Haven't heard much from you," said Jock, the wireless op.

"Well, you've been pretty quiet yourself."

"OK, fellows," Roper intervened, "quiet down and concentrate on watching out for fighters. There'll be enough time for chitchat later."

About twenty minutes later I advised Roper that we were well clear of enemy territory, so he was able to stop the tiring weaving pattern. From there on it was an uneventful flight back to base. At about 12:40 A.M. I asked Toddy to watch out for the English coast.

"Coastline coming up, Nav. We've made it," Toddy said a few minutes later, with barely suppressed excitement. But he wasn't any more excited than I was!

"Skipper, Navigator here. The 'drome is about ten minutes dead ahead. I doubt we are the first back, so the lights should already be on."

"Roger, Navigator."

Everyone, except Waggy, the rear gunner, and Jock, the wireless op, were looking ahead and wondering who would see the airfield lights first. I think we all saw them together as someone said, "There they are!"

"Hello, Bottie.[6] Hello Bottie. B-Bertie calling. B-Bertie calling. Requesting permission to pancake [land]. Over," Roper called the control tower.

"Hello, B-Bertie, this is Bottie calling. You may pancake. You may pancake."

"Hello Bottie, B-Bertie pancaking. Over."

While Roper circled into position for landing, Rosie switched on the landing lights and lowered the undercarriage. Then, following Roper's instruction, he began lowering the flaps.

Roper turned into the funnel of lights leading to the runway in use. Standing in my usual position behind the engineer, I saw the runway lights rushing up to meet us. A bump, and we were down. We had flown *into* hell, and now we were back home—*from* hell!

---

[1] The RAF equivalent of an army lieutenant colonel.

[2] The same rank as a major in the army.

[3] The RAF equivalent of an army colonel.

[4] Enemy night fighters.

[5] All details of flight times, heights flown, targets, dates, and other crew data, are factually accurate, the information having been obtained from squadron records and personal letters written at the time.

[6] Code name for Elsham Wolds airfield. Each bomber also had a code letter. Our Halifax was B-Bertie.

# BLACK OCTOBER

While Roper taxied to our dispersal point, the intercom came alive with the voices of different crew members excitedly recalling highlights of this, our first operation. Roper cut the throttles. We had been listening to the roar of the engines for hours, and the silence was profound. I paused a moment to absorb the peace and lack of noise; it was in such stark contrast to the violence of war that we had just experienced. Then, gathering my paraphernalia, I joined the rest of the crew on the tarmac, where we received warm congratulations from the ground crew.

"Everything go all right, Skipper?" asked Jim Baker, the sergeant in charge of our ground crew.

"Perfect, Chiefie," Johnny Roper replied. "They did a great job, didn't they, Rosie?"

"Couldn't have done a better job myself," responded Rosie, our flight engineer, with a grin.

We all knew how much our safety depended on the diligent efforts of the ground crew to maintain the aircraft at a high level of airworthiness. Often they worked tirelessly, without complaint, in foul weather conditions. Meanwhile, all of us except Johnny Roper had eagerly lit up our first cigarette in hours, enjoying the relaxation it brought us.

At the debriefing, exuberance grew as we learned that all the aircraft had returned safely. Accounts of hair-raising experiences followed, one after the other, as the airmen "became airborne again," as we referred to such bragging.

# SHOT DOWN!

*A Halifax ready for takeoff*

After debriefing, it was off to the mess for a meal and then to bed. I was glad that Johnny Roper and I shared a two-bed room to ourselves and therefore enjoyed a peace and quiet that wasn't always found in the larger barrack rooms.

Two nights later, on October 15, it was operations again, this time to Cologne in the heart of the heavily defended industrial Ruhr Valley. Twilight had spread across the airfield as we climbed aboard B-Bertie. We were somewhat subdued because we knew we were in for a tough night.

As the heavy-laden Halifax lumbered down the runway and grudgingly lifted into the darkening sky, I again experienced that feeling of exhilaration tempered with apprehension as I stood just behind Rosie. Then I returned to my cabin and entered the time of takeoff—1911 hours. We would be over our target in only two and a half hours. It seemed no time at all until we saw scores of searchlights stabbing the night sky ahead. And then we were in the midst of fury! To port, to starboard, ahead, and behind, the sky was continuously lit with exploding antiaircraft shells.

Then came the dreaded two minutes when Toddy said, "OK, Skipper, straight and level now. Bomb doors."

"Bomb doors open."

"Hold it steady, Skipper, we've got a good run onto the markers.[1] A little to starboard. That'll do. Steady, steady, bombs gone!" Still, the nerve-wracking straight-and-level flying had to be maintained until Toddy called out, "Photo taken." The words were barely out of his mouth before Roper pulled B-Bertie hard to port and, with violent evasive action, got us safely away from the target area.

Two and a half hours later, we landed. It was twenty minutes past midnight.

The debriefing room was filled with the usual haze of cigarette smoke and the sound of crews swapping yarns as each waited its turn for debriefing. But the conversations quieted down as one of the men called out, "Anyone seen Winchester? Are they back yet?"

"No. Neither is Parker," someone else replied.

Now we were all quiet. We looked at each other with dread in our minds and on our faces. Flight Lieutenant[2] K. F. J. Winchester, DFC,[3] and Flight Lieutenant G. N. Parker were two of our senior pilots. After debriefing, our crew and others hung around for any news. Finally, when no word was received that Winchester or Parker had landed at some other aerodrome, the crews were posted as missing. This was another bad night for the squadron, and a somber mood once more settled over us all.

A week had now gone by since I had returned late from my leave; I was beginning to wonder—to hope—it might be forgotten or overlooked. But no such luck. My flight commander, S/L Fox, took a dim view of such lack of discipline and decided to punish me by making me serve six consecutive nights as "aerodrome pilot," a post not nearly as glamorous as it might sound. Being "aerodrome pilot" meant being stationed for hours at the end of the runway, ready to operate an Aldis lamp[4] in case of an emergency. I never really understood what I was supposed to do. My six-night stint couldn't have come at a worse time. The weather had turned foul again and there were no operations for nine nights. Early signs of winter had come to this high, wind-swept wold, and my punishment was a bitterly cold and miserable experience. Ted Mawdsley's *An Erk's Eye View of World War II* poetically but accurately describes what the weather was like at Elsham Wolds at that time. "By mid-day the sullen, depressing clouds were no longer sulking over Lincolnshire, but were now hurtling like sky-grown tumbleweed towards the west, driven by a biting wind which had come, unopposed, all the way from Siberia." Six nights of that wind was tough, and I wasn't sure that the extra time at home was worth it.

# SHOT DOWN!

Even though my flight commander, Sid Fox, was himself only twenty-eight years old, he inspired trust and confidence. In spite of what I considered, at the time, to be rather harsh punishment, I still admired and respected him—as did all the airmen on our base. He helped me, still a teenager, to "find my feet" on the squadron. We looked up to him especially because he wore the ribbon of the highly prized Distinguished Flying Medal (DFM) which is awarded to airmen below the rank of commissioned officer. This indicated he had risen through the ranks from sergeant to squadron leader. (The equivalent of this medal for officers was the Distinguished Flying Cross [DFC] which was awarded more frequently even though there were far fewer commissioned officers than NCOs.) However, as I learned on this occasion, we did well to remember that he was now the senior flight commander and that he brooked no nonsense. He was a fairly strict disciplinarian, as my experience had shown.

For some time, we had been hearing about a superb new heavy bomber, the Lancaster, which some squadrons were already flying. On the morning of October 24 S/L Fox announced to the crews gathered at the squadron office that the 103rd Squadron would be converting to the Lancaster at the end of the month. We cheered loudly at the news. The rest of the day, we discussed the announcement excitedly. In fact, our discussions ended only when we received word later that afternoon that we would be flying missions that night.

At the briefing session we learned that our objective would be Milan in northern Italy. But as we settled into our places on board B-Bertie and Roper started up the engines, he found that all was not well with the plane. The oil pressure in one of the engines was low. After revving the engine for some time and consulting with Rosie, the flight engineer, Roper shut down the engines and informed the control tower that B-Bertie was unserviceable and that he was scrubbing the flight. We were somewhat disappointed because we had been led to believe that operations against Italian targets, though long, were less dangerous than those against German targets. Such raids were represented on the nose of the bombers with an ice-cream cone instead of a bomb.

After reporting back to the squadron office, we headed for the sergeants' mess. After a couple of hours, Roper and I decided to turn in for an early night. The next morning we learned the stunning news that S/L Fox and his crew were missing, as were also Sergeant S. A. Claridge and crew. The loss of Sid Fox left us all in deep shock. We had been at Elsham Wolds less than two months, and we had already lost twelve crews, including those of both flight commanders. More than half of these twelve crews had been our most experienced, top senior crews who were on their second tour of operations. According to official squadron records, of these eighty men who were shot down, sixty-three were killed.

For a while, I found myself wondering whether any of us would ever reach the magical number of thirty operations and leave the squadron alive. But I managed to subdue my fears and doubts with the firmly held belief that, although others might "get the chop," I and my crew would be among the lucky ones to make it through. I'm sure others thought the same. During the six and a half months that Johnny Roper and I shared our room, we never once talked about the possibility of being shot down. As crew after crew were listed as missing, we came to treat it with indifference. Was it just a mask or a reality? Maybe it was a bit of both.

Superstition played a prominent role in the lives of most airmen. Many wore lucky charms and firmly believed that those charms brought them back safely from a raid. I always wore a yellow woolen cravat covered with small fox heads that my sister Barbara had given me. I'm not sure if I really believed it was a lucky charm, but I was careful to wear it on every mission.

Sometimes we heard bizarre stories about green or brown gremlins, and the airmen who told these stories truly believed they had seen them dancing out on the wings of their planes. Green gremlins were friendly elves that helped the aircraft to fly safely; brown gremlins were evil elves who tried to make the plane crash. So said those who believed in them!

Much later, after the war had ended, I heard of a rear gunner in another squadron who wore one of his wife's silk stockings tied around his neck. He never took it off, not even in the shower. Only when his crew had successfully completed their tour of thirty operations did he remove it. And later in life he swore it was that stocking that got them through without being shot down. Such was the power of superstition with some of the men.

On October 28 we were again scheduled for operations. The target this time was the distant Baltic seaport of Stettin (now Szczecin) in Poland, an eight-hour trip that would require us to conserve fuel carefully even after taking on the maximum load we could carry. Of course, that also meant little margin for navigational error.

The meteorological report only heightened the deep concern we were all experiencing. Meredith, the senior meteorological officer, predicted low clouds over much of our route and the strong possibility that much of England would be blanketed with fog by the time we returned.

At this point Group Captain Constantine, the station commander, declared that if there were any probability that fog would require all aircraft to be diverted to Cornwall in the far west of England, he would not permit the squadron to take off.

Before the main briefing was over, the time of takeoff was postponed six hours, giving us time to take in the film being shown that evening in the squadron cinema. However, with the thought of this long and hazardous raid ever present on our minds, it wasn't easy to relax and really enjoy the film. This all changed when a voice declared over the loudspeaker: "All night flying has been cancelled! Repeat. All night flying has been cancelled!" After some loud spontaneous cheering, we all settled back to fully enjoy the film.[5]

Thus ended the brief, but very costly, three-month era of the Halifax bomber at the 103rd Squadron. But there were some "forgotten" men who were not in the warm comfort of the cinema, enjoying that film, but who were still out in the cold, miserable evening weather at the dispersal points. Hour after hour, these unsung ground crews had been keeping the bombers ready for takeoff at any time, pausing from time to time to swing their arms and beat their hands together to stimulate a little warmth. This would be repeated again and again during the coming winter months as operations would be scheduled and then cancelled due to bad weather. The air-crews would cheer as they settled down to comfortable evenings in their messes or take advantage of transport provided for an evening in Scunthorpe, but I doubt whether much thought was given to the "erks" who were out in the cold, faithfully keeping the bombers ready for takeoff should the operation not be cancelled. Truly their essential work on the squadron's aircraft was often very irksome; it was this that gave them the nickname of "erks."

---

[1] The markers were colored pyrotechnics dropped by Pathfinder bombers to mark the center of the target area. These bombers were equipped with special radar for this purpose.

[2] A Flight Lieutenant is the RAF equivalent of an army captain.

[3] The Distinguished Flying Cross.

[4] A hand-held, battery-operated lamp with a shutter by which messages could be flashed using Morse code.

[5] I have recollection of this operation being scheduled and later being scrubbed while we were in the cinema. However, for the details of that event, I am indebted to Don Charlwood and his excellent memoir of bomber command life at Elsham Wolds, *No Moon Tonight*.

# LANCASTERS AND A NASTY CLOUD

Two days later we awakened to a cold, miserable day. But in spite of the overcast sky and the rain, there was a peacefulness which belied the war raging in the Pacific theater where my cousin Michael Curnow, died with a thousand other men when his battleship was sunk by the Japanese. Or in North Africa where my brother-in-law Captain Peter Heddle was fighting with the British "Desert Rats" against the formidable German Afrika Corps. Or out in the Atlantic where enemy U-boats were sinking our merchant ships at an alarming rate.

After breakfast the quiet was broken by the sound of an approaching aircraft. The roar of its powerful engines grew louder and louder, and we watched the first of our new Lancaster bombers arrive. Cheers went up as it swooped down to make a graceful landing on one of our three runways.[1]

*The Lancaster bomber—queen of the skies!*

More Lancasters continued to arrive throughout the day, and the squadron's excitement grew. Finally quietness returned to Elsham Wolds in the late evening, as the last departing Halifax, piloted by one of the special "ferry" pilots who had delivered the Lancasters, rolled down the runway and took off into the still-overcast sky. Quiet returned, but the excitement remained, for we all believed that with the faster, more maneuverable Lancaster our heavy losses would be less. Sadly, S/L Sid Fox, who had announced barely a week earlier that we would be receiving the new Lancaster bombers, was not there to see it happen. Along with four of his crew, he now lay buried in the graveyard of a small French village, Nant-le-Grand.

I was reminded of his absence a few days later when I was hauled before S/L J. H. Kennard to face charges for having returned late from my leave. I stood at attention before him with my cap off and heard him pronounce the sentence of *Severe Reprimand*—a very serious punishment to have on one's service record.

Taking a deep breath, I said, "Excuse me, Sir, but I cannot be punished in this way!"

A look of surprise came over his face, followed by a flush of anger. "Indeed, Sergeant! And why not?" he demanded in a very sharp voice.

"With due respect, Sir," I replied, "Air Force law does not permit someone to be punished twice for the same offence, and I have already been punished by S/L Fox for returning late from my leave last month."

"What punishment did he give you?" S/L Kennard barked.

"Six consecutive nights on aerodrome pilot duty, Sir."

Kennard turned to the administration flight sergeant, who had marched me into his office, and asked whether that was correct.

"Yes, Sir," replied the flight sergeant.

With a frown and a look of chagrin on his face, my new flight commander snapped, "You are hereby admonished. Dismissed!"

"Yes, Sir!" I clicked my heels in salute, turned smartly, and left his office.

Outside the office, the flight sergeant said, "You're a smart one, pulling that off!"

"Flight, you know Air Force law," I replied. He nodded his head, and I breathed a big sigh of relief that an admonishment would not go onto my service record.

SHOT DOWN!

Like everyone else, our crew was impatient to get a closer look at the Lancasters. So as soon as Johnny Roper told us we had been assigned to D-Donald we all trooped out to our dispersal point in spite of the miserably cold, drizzly weather. And we liked what we saw!

We admired her sleek, graceful lines; just sitting on the runway she gave the impression of power and speed. I particularly liked the layout of the navigator's compartment with the wireless operator next to me on the left and a heavy curtain separating me from the pilot's cockpit to my right. We slapped each other on the back and told each other that the Jerries would rue the day they had started bombing London, Coventry, and other British cities. In a letter I wrote home on November 1, I gave my first impressions of this new plane:

> The squadron is now converting to a new kite, ten times better than the Halifax. It is the Lancaster, and are we pleased! The best way I can compare the two is, I think, by saying the comparison is like that of a racehorse to a carthorse, the "Lanc" being the racehorse.
>
> The weather here is positively rotten—rain and fog all the time and bitingly cold.

This November was also a very important time for a personal reason. Johnny Roper, a nonsmoker himself, challenged me to give up smoking. When I accepted, he turned around and offered to wager me one quid (an English pound) that I would smoke before the end of the month! A pound was a sizable amount of money at that time, representing about one-and-a-half day's pay.

At the end of the month, knowing that I was no longer smoking, Johnny held out a pound note and said, "Well done, John. I'm proud of you. Here's your quid."

"No, Johnny," I replied, refusing his money and pulling out a pound note myself. "Our bet wasn't that I would give up smoking, but that I would smoke before the end of the month. I smoked one cigarette later that first day. But it's worth this quid to give up smoking. Thanks for getting me to kick the habit." I know Johnny was very pleased that our room was now one of the few at Elsham Wolds that was smoke-free.

On November 21 I wrote home about a training flight which concluded our conversion to the Lancaster.

> Two days ago we (that is, the crew) went on an eight-hour cross-country flip; 1,480 miles right up to the very north of Scotland and half way to Iceland before we turned for home. We flew above 10/10 cloud all the time without seeing the deck. We lobbed down at an aerodrome near York as the cloud was down to 300 feet at base and we did not like the idea of coming down through it blind, bang next to the Hull balloon barrage. We trooped into Hull the next evening as we stayed there a couple of days, only coming back this morning.
>
> Do you know that that flip we did was further than Berlin and back, and as far as Italy and back. Boy, was I tired!

After two days, the weather cleared, and we were able to return to Elsham Wolds. The next night we received a briefing for a raid on Stuttgart, deep into Germany. All ten aircraft returned safely.

Except for two nights, bad weather kept the squadron grounded for the next two weeks. Our crew missed those two operations because we were on our next six-day leave. But when we returned to the squadron, we learned we had just lost our first Lancaster, piloted by Flying Officer Cumming. He was an experienced pilot, just starting his second tour, and this raid on Frankfurt was the crew's third operation. The mood at the squadron was pensive. Were we going to continue having heavy losses? Only time would tell.

Two nights later we were briefed for a raid on Mannheim. All twelve bombers from the 103rd Squadron returned safely. The following night just four crews went on a mine laying operation. The next night was, again, a mine laying operation, but this time the whole squadron was involved. However, for the second time we failed to take off because of oil pressure problems with the starboard engines. Our skipper, by nature a cautious pilot, very rightly would take off only if all four engines were functioning properly.

For the fourth night in a row the squadron was flying missions, briefed this time for a raid on Turin. This was our first trip to Italy, and, as we had been led to expect, we found the defenses of Turin pathetically inadequate. Though our bombers were flying well above the range of the light flak, the Italians kept firing scores of light antiaircraft guns anyway. The tracer shells clearly showed that the gunners below were just swinging their guns back and forth, randomly "hosing" the sky, with the tracer shells arcing over and falling back to earth. I had a bird's-eye view of this spectacular "fireworks" display; it almost made me feel guilty that we were bombing such a poorly defended target. We never saw anything like this over German cities.

In these four consecutive nights of operations we did not lose a single aircraft, and we began to feel that maybe the tide of heavy losses had turned with the arrival of the Lancasters. And squadron records would later show that the number of Lancasters being lost per one hundred sorties dropped to half that of the Halifaxes. We now had a glimmer of hope that completing a tour of thirty missions was possible.

December 9 saw a change in the command of Elsham Wolds. Group Captain H. A. Constantine, DSO (Distinguished Service Order), was posted to our Group Headquarters, and his place was taken by Group Captain L. W. Dickens, DFC, AFC (Distinguished Flying Cross, Air Force Cross).

Another week of bad weather grounded the squadron, but on December 17, Bomber Command called for another mine laying trip. The battle of the Atlantic was in full swing with German U-boats, operating out of French bases on the Atlantic seaboard, wreaking havoc on our vital supply lines. With these mine laying operations we were making it hazardous for the U-boats to leave and return to their bases.

Surprisingly, only one crew was detailed from Elsham Wolds for this mine-laying mission—our most senior crew, led by H. B. Smith. Smith had just been promoted from sergeant to pilot officer. His crew had begun its tour of duty back in early June—the old Wellington days before the squadron had converted to Halifaxes—and was the only one left from those times. Unfortunately, Smith and his crew did not make it back to base. It was later reported that they were shot down by a night fighter and were all killed.

With Christmas now only five days away, one topic for discussion in the mess was: "Would there be operations on Christmas Day?"

That night we were briefed for a raid on Duisburg. As I sat at my table making last minute adjustments to my flight plan, I heard Johnny Roper and Rosie discussing the starboard engine oil pressures. "Not again," I said to myself. Yes, once again Roper was not satisfied with the airworthiness of the plane and decided to scrub the flight. The next morning we learned that we had lost another of the old Halifax crews, led by Sergeant Moriarty.

Our latest scrub—the third since we had become operational—resulted in our skipper being called before the squadron commander later in the morning. When Roper came out from that unpleasant interview he was white-faced and tightlipped. He wouldn't tell us what W/C Carter had said to him, but we knew we were now under a cloud, suspected of lacking moral fiber and looking for any excuse to avoid going on an operation. We were very angry. It was tough enough flying into hell and back, without having this weighing on our minds. We were not the only crew that came under the lash of the commander's withering tongue.

But we couldn't allow ourselves to dwell on that; we had to move on. As I sat in the mess lounge, mulling over our squadron commander, my thoughts were broken by the crackle of the loudspeaker. Once again my stomach muscles knotted and my breathing became heavy as I heard the voice say: "Attention all aircrews! Attention all aircrews! There will be operations tonight." The usual instructions followed.

Looking around, I could tell that the other men were reacting the same way. A few tried to pass it off lightheartedly, but as they made their way to the bar and quickly downed a beer or whiskey, you could tell they were bluffing.

The operation that night was a long, seven-hour round trip to Munich deep in southern Germany. All went well for us on this mission, and we were the first to arrive back at base. It was during this period that Johnny Roper, Rosie the engineer, and I came up with a plan to get back to the aerodrome first. From then on we were always the first plane back from a mission—right up until our last operation.

How did we do it and why?

The prescribed procedure for leaving a target area was to throttle back a little for fuel conservation but to maintain the same speed by slowly losing altitude. With our plan, we maintained our bombing altitude, while still maintaining the cruising speed of 260 miles per hour. When we were about 80 miles from base I would advise Roper it was time to "put the nose down." At this time he would start losing altitude rapidly, and our speed would increase to 300 miles per hour or even more. This is how we pulled ahead of the other aircraft and arrived back at base first.

Having first used the G-Box[2] to obtain a good fix, I then used it as an accurate homing device, so that we arrived at the aerodrome on either the east or the northeast quadrant of the landing circuit, ready for an immediate landing when the aerodrome lights were switched on. There were several advantages for putting ourselves into this position. First, we were always able to land straight away without having to "stack." Each aircraft, when it arrived back at the base, was given an altitude at which to circle the aerodrome, with each plane five hundred feet above the previous arrival. Each aircraft would then drop down to the next level as the plane at the bottom of the stack landed. Sometimes the last aircraft to reach base had to circle for nearly half an hour before it was able to land.

Another advantage was that the transport picking up the crews always took the first crew straight to the ops HQ for debriefing, without waiting to pick up a second crew. After that the transport always picked up two crews at a time, which meant the second crew to arrive back had to wait for the third crew, and so on. By being the first ones back and getting into landing position, we never had to wait to be debriefed; often we would be finished and off to the dining room for a meal before the next two crews had even arrived.

This led to another big advantage. The cook would ask us whether there were any others on our heels. On the many occasions when we were able to answer "No," he would add eggs, bacon, and fried tomatoes to our meal. The other crews didn't know this! And often we were in bed asleep an hour before the last crew was heading for its quarters.

There was, however, a downside to this strategy: We missed the special camaraderie that prevailed as the crews swapped experiences while waiting for debriefing or having a meal together in the dining room. Because of this, I didn't get to know the other men in the squadron quite as well as I otherwise would have. I've sometimes wondered whether others thought we were a bit aloof. We weren't; we just thought that what we were doing was worth the benefits. My navigational log for the operation did not show this strategy.

The next morning we awoke to more bad news! Once again we had lost our senior crew, skippered by an Australian pilot, F/L J. C. Rose, who had been awarded the Distinguished Flying Cross (DFC) the previous month. Since he was a flight lieutenant, this indicated he and his crew were on their second tour, and with nineteen operations under their belt they had only six more to be finished for good. Rose and his crew were all killed. We also lost another of our four Australian pilots, Sgt. C. E. Bayliss. He and his crew had begun operations just two days after our crew, so we were particularly sorry to lose them. I know the remaining Australians felt the loss of half their pilots in one operation very keenly.

By an incredible miracle, Bayliss was the only survivor when his crew was shot down by a night fighter. When cannon shells ripped through the starboard wing, setting the plane on fire, Bayliss gave the order for the crew to bail out. Before heading for the emergency exit in the bomb aimer's compartment, Sergeant Nicholls, the engineer, stopped to clip Bayliss's parachute onto his harness. But before anyone could bail out, the Lancaster dived out of control, pinning them all in the death grip of powerful G-forces. On the way down to certain death for all of them, the fuel tanks in the starboard wing exploded and blasted Bayliss out of the doomed bomber. He came back to consciousness in time to open the parachute his engineer had so providentially clipped on for him. This amazing escape was to be repeated, almost identically, two-and-a-half months later. But more of that in chapter 10.

With Rose and Bayliss shot down, only five crews were left that had flown Halifaxes—those of F/L Douglas, F/S Newett, Sergeant Berry, F/S Austin, and my own crew. Would one of us break this disastrous spell in which no crew was making it through?

Two days later, on Christmas Eve, we were again briefed for operations. This time we learned we would be flying a long mission to Turin. At first there was a lot of grumbling because we would miss the Christmas Eve ball scheduled that evening at the sergeants' mess. But disappointment quickly turned to revelry when it was announced later that the operation had been cancelled.

Most airmen, whose lives revolved around violence and who were constantly facing sudden death, gave little thought to "peace on earth and good will to men" or to the Prince of Peace whose birth we were supposed to be celebrating. Rather, for many, it was a time to drown their fears and worries in free-flowing alcohol. I, too, celebrated Christmas Eve with the bottle, but I believe Johnny Roper kept me in check. Being as young as I was (and even younger than my companions realized), I could be fairly easily influenced by others in such social matters. Sharing a room with Johnny for more than six months was an influence on me for good. He got me to quit smoking, and he helped me not to go overboard drinking as so many of the fellows did. Though Johnny would have a drink now and then, I never saw him get even close to being drunk. He was a quiet, somewhat reserved, young gentleman. During those cold, dreary winter months when the squadron was grounded for days on end, instead of heading for the pubs in Scunthorpe, I would quite often grab my ice skates and, with Johnny, catch a bus to the coastal town of Grimsby, which had an ice rink.

The next day we awakened to a white Christmas. The blanket of new snow breathed the very essence of "peace on earth and good will to men." Somehow, it masked the violence and hate of which Elsham Wolds was a symbol. Those who attended the early morning carol service sang with gusto "I'm Dreaming of a White Christmas," along with many traditional carols.

The highlight of the day was lunchtime, when all the senior NCOs (sergeants and above) and officers made their way to the airmen's mess hall to serve the lower ranking men their Christmas lunch (those who were able to eat, that is, for some were dealing with heavy hangovers from the night before). This was a tradition that was observed each year. With plenty of beer readily available, some of the "waiters" had crashing accidents as they carried loaded trays. The station, squadron, and flight commanders all joined in; for a while, all thoughts of rank were forgotten.

After Christmas, overcast, foggy weather settled back over much of England, making it unsuitable for night flying. But early in the new year the weather cleared, and on January 4 we were back in the thick of the deadly task of helping to destroy Hitler's evil Nazi regime. Our target was Essen, in the heart of Germany's industrial Ruhr. We all returned safely!

A couple of days later it was our turn, again, for six days leave. Since it was winter and all my friends at Ickenham were away in the armed forces, these six days were a time for me to stay in bed late and enjoy my mother's great cooking!

Back at Elsham Wolds, we learned that the squadron had been busy pounding Essen. During our leave, four operations had taken place against this heavily defended city. The squadron had flown thirty-five sorties and had lost two rookie crews, both of which were shot down on their third operation. Of these fourteen men, only Sgt. A. S. Laird, one of the two navigators, survived.

January 16, we were briefed for the "Big City," Berlin. Again our crew's troubles began. One by one, the other ten Lancasters taxied to the runway and took off, while we sat at our dispersal point with Roper revving that troublesome starboard engine with low oil pressure. Finally, a voice from the control tower radioed, "Calling D-Donald. You are now twenty minutes late, and the last aircraft has taken off. Either proceed immediately to the runway for takeoff or scrub."

Knowing what would be in store if he scrubbed, but with considerable reluctance, Roper replied, "Hello, Bottie. D-Donald calling. The oil pressure in the starboard inner has come up, and we're proceeding to runway for takeoff. Over."

While taxiing to the runway we were instructed not to circle the aerodrome to gain altitude, but to climb en route. I hurriedly worked out a new course so that we flew directly out over the North Sea, bypassing the rendezvous point at Skegness. Roper opened the throttles wider so we would catch up with the main force before crossing the enemy coast.

When we arrived at Berlin nearly four hours later the raid was well under way with many fires burning below. As we flew into the violent battle zone, my heart began to pound. Meanwhile, Toddy had left the front gun turret and had taken up his bomb-aiming position. As we neared the center of the target zone for the potentially deadly two minutes of straight-and-level flying for the bombing run, I found myself gripping the back of the pilot's seat and the side of the fuselage so tightly my knuckles were white.

The "Big City," as we called Berlin, was fighting back vigorously. Scores of searchlights stabbed the night sky, and we heard the "crump" of nearby exploding antiaircraft shells. Finally Toddy was satisfied with his aim, released the bombs, and then reported the photo taken. Pulling D-Donald on a tight banking turn to port, Roper cleared the target area with the usual strong evasive action and then settled into the regular weaving pattern as he headed for the North Sea.

Only when I returned to my navigation chart and log, did my heart begin to calm down. Berlin was a frightening target!

Following our plan, we maintained our bombing height of eighteen thousand feet until we were about eighty miles from base, at which time I said over the intercom, "OK, Skipper, you can put the nose down."

I entered into the G-Box the two radar coordinate numbers for the northeast quadrant of the squadron's outer ring of landing lights. I then switched to the other screen which showed the two blips, one on one side of the screen, and one on the other side. As I watched them slowly move toward the fixed center blip, I periodically gave small corrections to Roper so that the two moving blips would arrive at the center at the same time. When they were quite close I told him to be ready to call the control tower. Finally, when the three blips were on top of each other, I said, "OK, Skipper, call up."

All was dark below as Roper called the control tower, asking for permission to land. Over the radio came the voice of a young WAAF (Women's Auxiliary Air Force), saying those words which spoke of life and safety to every returning air-man: "You may pancake." At the same time the airfield lights came on, showing the funnel to be less than half way around the outer ring of lights.

"I think I can make it, Engi-neer," Roper said. "Quick. Un-dercarriage down. Flaps down," he snapped as he pushed the nose down, losing three or four hundred feet rapidly. With the entrance to the funnel rushing toward us, I braced myself against the centrifugal pull as Johnny leveled off and made a tight turn into its mouth. By the way he was handling D-Donald you'd have thought he had for-gotten that he had transferred from Fighter Command to Bomber Command and was no

*The voice speaking the words every airman wanted to hear: "You may pancake!"*

longer in the cockpit of a Spitfire or Hurricane!

As we trooped into the debriefing room we knew immediately that something was wrong. Instead of greeting us cordially, the in-telligence officer watched us in silence as we wearily sat down. After a moment of silence he started asking questions we didn't expect for a normal debriefing.

"Gentlemen, you were very late in taking off. How late were you getting to the target?" Not waiting for an answer, he continued in a challenging tone of voice, "How have you managed to arrive back so early, *if* you made it all the way to the target?"

"What do you mean, *if?*" Roper asked in a low voice of controlled anger.

"Gentlemen, I will be frank with you. You took off more than half an hour after the first aircraft, and yet you have returned so early the next plane has not yet arrived back. We are questioning whether you have actually been to the target."

"What!" we chorused with angry disbelief.

"Get the photo developed," Toddy, our usually quiet bomb aimer, exclaimed heatedly. "That will prove we bombed Berlin!"

Eyeing Toddy intently, the officer asked doubtfully, "Were you flying straight and level for a good photo?"

"We always fly straight and level for the bombing run," Roper spat out the words with his fists clenched so tightly his knuckles were white.

Sensing the level of tension and our intense anger, the officer stood up, saying, "All right, gentlemen. But I will have to ask you wait in another room until the photo is developed." He then led us to an adjacent room. We waited in stunned silence for over half an hour, unable to believe that we were virtually under house arrest.

Finally the officer entered the room with a puzzled look on his face. "Gentlemen, we don't understand it. Your photograph is an excellent one, and we have been able to plot it two miles east of the center of the target area. We apologize for doubting you. You did a great job!" Giving us each a warm handshake, he said we could go. We kept quiet about staying up at eighteen thousand feet on the way home, where we had obviously encountered a much more favorable wind. With lightened spirits we walked to the dining hall. We knew the cloud of doubt and suspicion under which we had been was now gone.

---

[1] The three runways were laid out in a triangle, which gave six different directions for takeoffs and landings. The wind direction determined which runway was used.

[2] The G-Box was a radar receiver which picked up signals transmitted from two locations in England. The signals appeared as two blips on the radar screen. By turning two knobs these blips were brought to the central fixed blip. Throwing a switch produced another screen on which the blips appeared as numbers. On a special chart these numbers were represented by two curving lines, and the position of the aircraft was the spot where those lines crossed. By reversing the process, the G-Box could be used as an accurate homing device.

# CRASH ON TAKEOFF

The next day there was good news and bad news! The good news was that all eleven of our bombers had made it safely back to base; the bad news was that we would raid Berlin again that night.

For this raid, our route took us across the Danish peninsula to the Baltic Sea. When we were due north of Berlin, we were to turn south and arrive to the east of the "Big City." As we approached the target area, I left my navigator's cabin and stood in the cockpit as was my custom. What I saw caused my heart to race. We were flying into an ominous trap. Scores of searchlights pointed straight up into the sky so that their widening beams were touching at seven thousand or eight thousand feet. We couldn't fly around these searchlights, for they stretched away in both directions; we had to fly through them!

Our hearts pounded, and fear dried our mouths and tightened our stomach muscles as we drew nearer to that deadly wall of light. Just when it seemed we would be nakedly exposed to deadly peril, the wall parted in front of us. Several of the searchlights had swung to starboard to home in on another bomber that had penetrated that blinding light display.

As we flew through the gap in front of us, I saw the pilot of the bomber that had been caught in the searchlights put his plane into a steep dive, trying to escape the light before the antiaircraft guns opened up on what was now a very visible target. Moments later my attention was riveted on a frightening sight ahead and to port.

Another bomber had been pinpointed in seven or eight searchlights, and a battery of antiaircraft guns began firing rapid salvos in such a way that the shells exploded at the same time. We called this "firing in a box." In the glare of the searchlights I saw the gray puffs of smoke from one salvo burst about a hundred feet below that hapless bomber. A few seconds later another salvo exploded much closer; the master gunner below was finding the range.

Then, in fascinated horror, I saw the third salvo explode all around the ill-fated bomber. There was a brilliant flash as at least one shell made a direct hit. Maybe a fuel tank exploded. For a moment the doomed bomber hung in the sky. Then, like a flaming meteor, it plunged earthward in a fiery blaze, taking its seven-man crew with it to their deaths. That was the only time I ever saw a bomber shot down, and the picture is imprinted vividly in my memory forever!

As that scene of death passed from my vision on the port side, Toddy's voice came over the intercom, "OK, Skipper, bomb doors."

"Bomb doors open," Roper replied. He stopped weaving and started flying straight and level. The thought flashed through my mind, *Was that ill-fated bomber flying straight and level when caught in the searchlights?*

*"Flare Takeoff." Drawn in my wartime log by POW artist Ray.*

I kept my eyes peeled for any lethal beam of light that might threaten us as Roper concentrated on keeping D-Donald flying straight and level. The nerve-wracking bombing run seemed to stretch on and on until we felt, again, the upward leap of the plane as eight thousand pounds of bombs dropped away. A few seconds later came Toddy's announcement for which we were all waiting so tensely: "Photo taken, Skipper. Let's get out of here!"

I hung on as Roper banked hard to starboard, away from the target area. All the time we kept our eyes skinned for night fighters. Just as we sometimes saw a night fighter flying beneath us, silhouetted against the fires burning below, so a night fighter flying above us might see us silhouetted against those same fires.

Once away from Berlin, Roper settled into a steady weaving pattern as we headed for the comparative safety of the North Sea. But we were not yet free from the danger of searchlights. As we were approaching the enemy coastline, Roper exclaimed over the intercom, "Look ahead!"

I went into the cockpit area and saw another wall of searchlights. However, once again, before we reached this second trap, the searchlights parted as they focused on another bomber flying some thousand feet below us to starboard. That pilot put his bomber into a steep dive, and the last I saw of it was the light flak tracer bullets coming from all directions. Judging by the almost horizontal trajectory of the flak, the bomber must have been barely above the treetops. I hoped the crew made it out over the North Sea, as we did shortly after.

Once again we covered the last eighty miles at a good three hundred miles per hour. After a quick debriefing and a tasty meal, I threw myself onto my bed without undressing and fell into a deep sleep.

The latter half of January continued to be a busy time for the squadron. Besides the two raids on Berlin, we also attacked Essen and Dusseldorf twice before being briefed for Hamburg. Coming in to land after the first raid on Dusseldorf, we ran into trouble. When Rosie lowered the undercarriage, he noticed the red warning light came on, indicating that the undercarriage was not locked in the "down" position.

"It may be only an electrical fault," Roper suggested. "Let's see if the hooter¹ comes on."

Entering the funnel of lights leading to the runway, Roper throttled back. As the runway lights came up to meet us, the hooter started blaring! Prepared for this, Roper immediately pulled up away from the runway and began climbing. He reported our problem to the control tower. The tower told us we would have to wait for the rest of the squadron to land, just in case ours would turn into a belly landing. Roper was instructed to stay five hundred feet above the last plane in the stack. By this time the other six bombers that had been on this raid began arriving.

Finally the last of the six planes was on the ground, and we received permission to land. Dobie, the wireless operator, Rosie, and I took up our crash-landing positions just in case the undercarriage collapsed when touching down. Fire trucks were standing by. Tension mounted as the blaring sound of the hooter filled the plane in the final stage of what turned out to be a perfect three-point landing! The trouble was nothing more than a simple electrical failure.

That wasn't the end of problems with our plane, however. We continued to have trouble with starboard engine oil pressures, though we didn't have to scrub any missions. But our problems came to a dramatic and potentially lethal climax during our takeoff for a raid against Hamburg. As we began gathering speed down the runway, the plane started to drift to port due to a strong crosswind. The more our speed accelerated, the more the drift increased, but the plane was still not moving fast enough for it to respond to the rudder. By the time Roper had corrected the drift, using the throttles, D-Donald had drifted off the runway onto the grass. We were now running parallel with the lighted runway! Roper was faced with a critical decision. Would there be enough time to stop before plunging into a fifty-foot-deep chalk pit that lay ahead in the darkness? Or was there still enough time to take off? Not having the runway lights to guide him, it was hard to judge. He decided to try to take off.

We were now going fast enough that he could control the plane with the rudder. So Roper equalized the throttles of the four engines and then eased them forward until the bomber was traveling at about eighty miles per hour, at which point he pushed the four throttle leavers "through the gate" for the extra power available for takeoffs and emergencies. Both starboard engines died!

With both port engines at full throttle and with no power on the starboard side, the aircraft went into a crablike motion, putting such a strain on the undercarriage that the starboard side collapsed. As the starboard wingtip dug into the soft ground, the fully laden bomber went into a flat spin, leaving a trail of wreckage. It passed directly across the runway and careened across the airfield. Since Rosie and I were both standing, it took all our strength to hang on and not be thrown around the cockpit.

Somehow Roper was able to reduce the power to the port engines, but only after D-Donald—or what was left of it—came to a juddering, lurching stop was he able to turn off these two engines completely. Why the Lancaster didn't burst into a ball of fire baffled us; as was their na-

*A photograph of the Elsham Wolds airfield taken on June 26, 1943, from 10,000 feet. The cross, right center, marks the place where we crashed.*

ture, the two hot Merlin engines belched flame from their exhausts as they coughed to a stop, while at the same time the air was reeking with the fumes of high octane aviation fuel spewing from ruptured fuel lines on the starboard side!

Jettisoning the escape hatch above his head, Roper climbed onto the port wing and jumped to the ground, closely followed by Rosie and myself. Todd exited through the bomb aimer's escape hatch, while the remaining three crew members went out through the main entrance. I have never run as fast as I did from that wreck! We expected it to be engulfed in flames at any moment. But except for the pounding of our feet on the turf and the sound of departing bombers overhead the silence was eerie.

Finally, when we realized that the plane was not going to catch fire, we stopped and slowly made our way back to our wrecked D-Donald, breathing heavily.

We could hardly believe what we saw. Fuel was still dripping from broken lines; there was only a gaping hole where the outer starboard engine had once been; the inner engine was hanging down, resting on the ground; the starboard undercarriage was completely gone, as were the starboard oil tank, fin and rudder, and the end section of the wing. The bomb-bay with its four thousand–pound blockbuster bomb and four thousand pounds of incendiary bombs was still intact. Only a miracle had averted a major disaster to the squadron!

The next morning we had a big laugh, although a somewhat nervous one, when we heard how everyone in the control tower had thrown themselves flat on the floor when they saw our lights spinning across the airfield. We also learned that three other bombers had not been able to take off due to our accident.

Hamburg was the last operation for Douglas, Newett, and Berry in the 103rd Squadron, as the next day they and their crews transferred to Pathfinders before finishing their tour of thirty operations. This left Bunny Austin's crew and ours as the last of old "Halibag" squadron crews still at Elsham Wolds. In these past five months we had seen fifteen Halifax crews lost, plus five Lancaster crews. But the tide *was* turning.

---

[1] A loud warning that sounded when the plane's speed dropped to near stalling speed, which, of course, was the case when landing. However, when the wheels were down and locked into position, this hooter was not activated.

# ALPINE EXCURSION

February 1943 saw the beginning of a heavy and sustained bombing offensive against the enemy. Altogether, the squadron was on operations twelve nights that month. Our crew missed the first three since we were without an aircraft, but a week after the crash we received a brand-new Lancaster with the same code letter "D." This letter led to an unresolved tussle with the people in the control tower. So far, the code letter "D" had always been referred to as D-Donald, but shortly after we got our new plane, either the squadron or the RAF decided to change it to D-Duck, which we didn't like. So whenever it was time to land Johnny Roper would continue to identify our plane as D-Donald, and the WAAF in the control tower would reply with D-Duck, putting emphasis on "Duck." In response Johnny would again use "Donald," but this time stressing the word just as strongly as the control tower had emphasized "Duck." Neither side gave in!

When we got our new Lancaster, the first thing I did was to paint the voluptuous figure of the goddess Diana on the port side of the nose of the plane. It was the same emblem I had previously painted on our wrecked Lancaster.

We were back into the full swing of operations. In six days we flew missions to Wilhelmshaven, Milan, Italy, and twice to the U-boat pens at Lorient in France. Our count was now sixteen operations—more than half of the seemingly unobtainable number of thirty. Would we make it? Bunny Austin and his crew, who had started with the squadron just eight days before us, were up to twenty-three. Everyone was now counting on them to break the bleak six-month spell during which no crew had been able to complete a full tour of thirty operations and leave Elsham Wolds alive.

Our first raid on the U-boat pens at Lorient, on the Atlantic coast of France, went well until our return to base. Arriving back at Elsham Wolds, Roper called up Bottie in the usual way, but there was no response; everything remained dark below. After two or three further attempts at calling the control tower failed to produce any response, we realized our radio was dead. Since we were flying toward Hull we started to hear, on our radio, the howling of the balloon barrage warning. This meant that only our transmitter was dead, not our receiver. To stay clear of the dangerous barrage, I told Roper to turn west for one minute, then south for a minute, then east for a minute, all the time monitoring our position on the G-box.

By then the second plane arrived and called in. Immediately the lights came on and F-Freddy was given permission to land. One by one the remaining eight planes returned and were given a height at which to fly. Each time we climbed to five hundred feet above the last plane. Then, as each plane landed we dropped down five hundred feet until the last plane was down. Then the unbelievable happened; the 'drome lights were turned off!

Since we could no longer circle the 'drome visually, we started flying that square pattern again. With D-Donald lined up with the airfield by means of the G-box, Roper roared low across the landing area with all our lights on. There was still no response from below.

By this time we were all getting very angry. Using our Aldis lamp, I started flashing our aircraft identification in what I believed was the direction of the airfield. Still no response from below! The control tower knew two planes had not landed; here was one roaring across the airfield with its lights on! (Besides ours, the other plane turned out to have been shot down on the mission; it belonged to P/O J. Young, an Australian, and his crew.) The idiot who was in charge of landings needed a spell of trench digging!

The next time around, as we flew low over the airfield, Roper instructed me to fire some signal cartridges, using the Veri pistol fixed in the roof of the cabin. Only after I fired the third cartridge were the lights turned on; we finally landed almost an hour after our initial arrival. In debriefing, Roper lost his temper and gave a blistering tirade about incompetence and the fact that we had been running low in fuel. After the control officer offered some apologies and lame excuses, our skipper finally calmed down.

Our operation to Milan the next night turned out to be a real challenge for me. All went well as we flew south over France, until the Pathfinders dropped the special pyrotechnic markers for the bombers to turn east toward the target. I was surprised that we had reached the turning point so soon and discussed it with Roper. We decided that since the Pathfinders had advanced radar navigational equipment we should follow their directive and turn east.

We had been heading east only a short while when Toddy said, "Hey, there are lights below. What kind of blackout is that?"

Moments later Rosie burst out, "Look, there's a lighted train!"

Meanwhile, I had gone into the cockpit to see for myself. "Good grief," I exclaimed. "We're over Switzerland!" We now realized the Pathfinders had goofed up.

"OK, Navigator, what do we do now?" Roper asked somewhat urgently. "We can't turn around and fly against other kites that may be behind us, and I don't feel like heading north into Germany."

"Give me a few minutes," I replied. "The Alps are well silhouetted in the moonlight. Let me see if I can pinpoint just where we are and find a pass low enough that we can cross into Italy." We were flying a little above fourteen thousand feet.

"OK, Navigator, but be quick about it, we've got to get out of Switzerland fast. This is a neutral country!"

Since we were over Switzerland we could safely have the cockpit lights on. This enabled me to read my topographical map, and scan the mountains at the same time. My task was to look at the mountain peaks silhouetted in the moonlight to the south, and then mentally turn those slopes into contour lines. Then, conversely, I had to look at the contour lines on the topographical map and turn them into a picture of sloping mountainsides, remembering that the steeper the slope the closer together the contour lines on the map and the gentler the slope, the wider apart were the lines.

"How's it going, Navigator?"

"I'm working on it, Skipper."

A couple of minutes later I said, "OK, Skipper, I know where we are."

"Are you absolutely sure?"

"Without any doubt."

"Good show! When do I turn?"

"We're coming up on a low area, so be ready to turn when I tell you."

"Roger, Navigator."

"OK, Skipper, see that high peak over there?" I asked, pointing about two o'clock. "And further east there is a lower peak. Do you see them?"

"Yep, I've got them," Roper replied.

"OK, we're going to turn in between them."

When we were level with the low area between the two peaks I told Roper to head for it. After a few minutes, he said, "Navigator, are you absolutely sure you know where we're going? Look at that peak dead ahead! Soon we'll be too close to those mountains for me to turn around."

"Yes, I know about that mountain. A little bit farther, you will see it drop off to the east. When you see that, turn a little to port. Then we'll be through them. Trust me; we're OK!"

If I'm wrong, we're dead! I told myself.

The taller peak I had pointed to was, I believe, Weisshorn, 14,782 feet high, while the one Roper had his eye on was Matterhorn, 14,679 feet high.

It was a nail-biting situation as we got closer and closer to the mountains. For a while, as the ground below us got ever higher, it looked as if we were lower than the saddle we were heading for. "I hope Curnow knows what he's doing!" Waggy, the rear gunner, said nervously.

In the front turret Toddy quipped, "What are you worrying about, Waggy? I'm the one who will hit the mountain first!"

This caused a laugh. A few moments later Roper banked slightly to port. We cleared the saddle by several hundred feet, and the snow below us dropped quickly away. Soon we were south of the Alps and over northern Italy, heading for Milan.

On our return flight we had our first and only encounter with a German night fighter, and a strange encounter it was!

Somewhere over northern France, Waggy, our ever-watchful rear gunner, broke the silence. "Bandit! Bandit!" he called out urgently. "Bandit at five o'clock and below!" He quickly turned his gun turret and trained his four machineguns on the approaching night fighter.

"How close is it? Roper asked tensely.

"Still out of range," Waggy replied. "Now what's he doing? He's cutting across to port and climbing. Do you see him, Mid-upper?"

"Yep, I have him," Ron May, our temporary mid-upper gunner replied, as he, too, got the fighter in the sights of his two machineguns. (Duncan, our regular mid-upper gunner was ill.)

"He's flying alongside us now; what on earth is he up to?" Rosie exclaimed excitedly.

"Everyone keep your eyes skinned for another fighter; he may be a decoy!" Roper barked. "And gunners, hold your fire. Our guns are for defense, not attack,"

Standing in the cockpit, I could see the single-engine fighter flying at the same speed and altitude as we, but out of range.

The fighter pilot continued his strange behavior for about ten seconds before peeling off in a tight, diving turn to port, rapidly disappearing from sight.

"Keep your eyes skinned," Roper said sharply. "We don't know what the Jerries may be up to." But we had no further contact with the enemy.

We often pondered this strange behavior, speculating that the fighter pilot had run out of ammunition and was just having a bit of risky fun with us. Though he was out of range for a sure hit, there was still a slender chance we could have gotten him with all eight Browning machineguns, each pumping twenty bullets a second. Just a short three-second burst would have poured 480 bullets at him!

After the war, I read, in a book about the Lancaster bomber, the comments of a German night fighter ace who said that German pilots had the highest regard for the Lancaster's defenses; once they knew they had been spotted by a bomber, they would not press the attack, but would go looking for another victim. Maybe, in the moonlight, our German night fighter pilot had seen our gun turrets turned in his direction!

Whatever that pilot's motive, the incident remains as a strange and vivid experience in my memory.

Soon we crossed the English Channel and were back over England. At debriefing we learned that the Swiss government had already lodged a strong protest in London against the violation of their neutrality. We also learned that only a few other bombers had been duped by the Pathfinder error. The bombers up ahead were not affected by the markers that were dropped behind them, of course. And most of the bombers behind us stayed on the correct course because the wrongly placed markers

*Left: F/L Meriel (Curnow) Heddle. Right: F/O Barbara Curnow and F/L John Curnow. Photos taken in 1945.*

were allowed to burn out without being replaced with new ones. Our plane and a few other aircraft were at the right place but at the wrong time!

The next day I was relaxing in the sergeants' mess lounge when I heard over the loudspeaker: "Sergeant John Curnow to report to the administration office. Repeat, Sergeant John Curnow to report to the administration office."

A couple of fellows nearby looked at me questioningly. I shrugged my shoulders. I didn't have a clue what it was about. I knew I hadn't been into any mischief.

Arriving at the administration office, I asked the flight sergeant what was up.

"You have an appointment to see the Groupie," he replied.

"Group Captain Dickens? Whatever for?"

"Interview for a commission," Flight said.

Caught completely by surprise, I said, "What! Me for a commission?" I had never even dreamed of such a thing.

"Yes, Curnow. Carter passed through a recommendation. Your interview is at 1500 hours. Don't be late—and good luck!"

I left the office with my head spinning. *Me,* the kid navigator on the squadron, recommended by the squadron commander, without even applying!

I told Johnny Roper about it over lunch. "You deserve it, John," he responded.

"No more than you, Johnny!" I replied, and I meant it. Johnny was a great pilot and just the officer type.

Did I detect a little sadness in his voice as he said with finality, "Carter will never recommend me for a commission, that's for certain." After his run in with the Winco and our crash on takeoff he firmly believed this.

Before heading for the station commander's office I spruced up and tried to calm down.

Promptly at three o'clock I knocked on the Groupie's door. Hearing "Come in," I took a deep breath, removed my cap, and entered. I came to attention and clicked my heels smartly in salute.

"Stand easy, Curnow."

After a short pause Group Captain Dickens asked, "What do you think about having this interview?"

"Bowled over, Sir," I replied.

A half smile came on his face. "What school did you go to?"

"The City of London, Sir."

"You had an Officers' Training Corps (OTC) at that school, didn't you?" the Groupie asked.

"Yes, Sir. Every Monday was OTC day, when we would be in army uniform."

"Why did you join the RAF?"

I paused a moment, then replied, "I joined the Home Guard when it was still the Land Defense Volunteers. And when I was on guard duty in my village west of London, I often saw the eastern sky turn red as the fires raged. I joined the RAF for revenge, Sir. Revenge for what the Germans were doing to London."

Another pause as Groupie looked at me. "Are you ever afraid, Curnow?"

"Who wouldn't be, Sir?"

Groupie held my gaze for a moment, then, with a slight nod of his head, said, "All right, Curnow. I'll be passing along my recommendation to Group Headquarters."

"Thank you, Sir," I responded, and the interview was over. I came to attention, clicked my heels in salute, turned, and left the room.

Confirmation of my commission would take several weeks; meantime I continued to carry the rank of sergeant. However, my service record shows I was discharged from the RAF on February 15, 1943, "having attained the rank of sergeant," and then commissioned back into the RAF the next day with the rank of pilot officer. I had now joined my two sisters as officers. They were both officers in the WAAF. We were a Royal Air Force family!

After a raid on the U-boat pens at Lorient the next night, it was home again for another six-day leave, when I could try to forget about war.

# APPOINTMENT WITH DEATH!

I came back to the squadron to find that no crews had been lost while I was on leave. In fact, in the ninety-nine sorties that the squadron had flown in the past five weeks, only two crews had been lost. There was a decided feeling of optimism as the squadron looked to the five senior crews, who had started back in 1942, to break the spell and complete a full tour of thirty operations. The five pilots were Bunny Austin, Johnny Roper, Syd Cook, Jock Greig, and Geoff Maddern.

The next night we were back into the thick of operations with four sorties—Nuremberg, Cologne, St. Nazaire, and Berlin—scheduled for the next five nights. We awakened the morning after the Berlin raid to learn that Bunny Austin and his crew had failed to return. Their loss, on their twenty-ninth operation, hit our crew particularly hard, for we had been with them in the squadron since the previous August. We were now the last of the old Halifax crews.

Another experienced crew, on their second tour, was also lost that night. A somber mood settled back on the squadron.

Two nights later the raid was on the important industrial city of Hamburg. This was our fifth operation in seven nights, and we were starting to feel a certain level of fatigue. We were happy, therefore, to be the first plane back—once again—and to get through debriefing without any delay. Then it was off for a quick meal and to bed. We awakened later in the morning to learn that another of the five senior crews had been shot down. Jock Greig and his crew were lost on their twentieth operation.

Now only three senior crews were left—Cook's, Maddern's, and our crew piloted by Johnny Roper. The rest of the squadron was comprised of relatively new crews. Three had been at Elsham Wolds for about six weeks; the rest had been in the squadron less than one month. However, the pilot of at least one of those new crews was starting his second tour of operations and had a lot of operational experience.

Later that day the squadron experienced a tragic accident when an engine on Lancaster W4333, piloted by F/O Nebojsa Kujundzic, caught fire while on a routine training flight. The fire extinguisher built into the engine successfully put out the fire, but then it reignited, whereupon the pilot ordered the crew to bail out.

Because they were over a populated area, the pilot stayed at the controls in order to guide the crippled Lancaster clear of Yaxley Village. By the time the plane was clear of the houses, it was too low for the pilot to bail out, and he died in the crash. Kujundzic, a twenty-five-year-old seasoned Serbian pilot, died a true war hero, far from his native Yugoslavia, willingly giving his life to save unknown English villagers!

The next night was the beginning of what became known as the Battle of the Ruhr—a prolonged series of devastating attacks on the industrial heartland of Germany using a new top secret device code named Oboe. This system depended on two radio stations in England both transmitting narrow radio beams that could be laid across the target with extreme accuracy. The aiming point for the bombers was the intersection of these two beams.

Our crew, along with nine others from the 103rd Squadron, were among the 442 aircraft detailed for the opening attack of the Battle of the Ruhr, which was to last some five months and result in heavy losses on both sides. Our target for this operation was the massive Krupps industrial complex at Essen. The accuracy of Oboe allowed us to inflict very heavy damage on the target.

After only a single night's unbroken sleep, we were detailed for the long seven-and-a-half-hour trip to Nuremberg. This and the

Essen raid were carried out without further losses among the crews in our squadron. But now a new enemy was stalking the grounds of Elsham Wolds—fatigue. Bunny Austin's crew had been shot down on their tenth operation in only nineteen days! Was fatigue a major factor? Nobody could be certain, for the plane was lost without a trace, no doubt over the North Sea.

*Headline in a London evening newspaper reporting an attack on Munich.*

The following night, March 9, we were again on operations, our eighth in thirteen nights, and our twenty-fourth over all. We would be starting out on a long eight-hour trip to Munich already tired. We were sitting on our parachute packs at our dispersal point, waiting for the ground crew to finish some maintenance work, when Flying Officer Henderson, one of the squadron's doctors, drove up. Seeing some of us sitting with our heads resting in our cupped hands, Dr. Henderson questioned our fitness to fly. "You fellows look pretty tired. I could stand you down, you know."

"No, Doc," Roper said, speaking for all of us. "Operations are moving along too well. Let's not break the run."

Looking around at us in silence, he finally said, "OK, if you feel sure you're up to it. Good luck, men."

"We'll be fine," Roper said as Doc Henderson turned away and walked slowly back to his car. He paused, his hand on the door handle, and took a final look in our direction. Then he was gone into the darkness.

The ground crew finished their work, and we climbed aboard. The surge of adrenalin that I always experienced on takeoffs drove any tiredness away, and I settled down to my navigation. A little more than three-and-a-half hours later we reached the turning point for the final run to Munich. Our run-in for the bombing was straightforward, and the only thing of note was a massive explosion on the ground. I had never before seen such a huge fireball.

As we left the target area, I returned to my navigating table. Suddenly, an overwhelming tiredness hit me; the mental fatigue that had been slowly building up for a week had now reached a peak. My navigational chart started to swim in front of my eyes; I couldn't focus on it. I chewed one of the large white caffeine tablets we carried to combat tiredness. I had never used one before so I didn't know how well it would work. It didn't work at all! My head drooped to the table, and I fell into a deep sleep. (Many years later, when I told a doctor about this experience, he said that taking a large dose of caffeine could have a drugging effect on some people. I don't know whether this was the case with me.)

A loud explosion ringing in my ears caused me to sit up with a start. I felt the plane shudder. My mind was now crystal clear, and instinctively I knew we had received a direct hit from an antiaircraft shell. As I jumped up, I grabbed my parachute and clipped it onto the harness I was wearing. Never before had I worn my parachute clipped on while flying. Disconnecting my oxygen line and unplugging my intercom, I moved into the pilot's cabin. Rosie was not at his usual station so I connected to his oxygen supply point and plugged into his intercom socket. D-Donald was flying normally, with the four powerful Merlin engines running smoothly. There appeared to be no immediate crisis.

"Where's Rosie?" I asked.

"Gone below," Roper replied.

On the starboard side of the cabin, below the pilot's control panel, was a narrow opening with two or three steps leading down to the bomb aimer's area where he would lie in a prone position to drop the bombs. I glanced down into the darkened area but saw nothing. No doubt Rosie had gone down to check the fuel line controls.

Roper was speaking again, "Take a look at the starboard wing and see what the damage is. We were hit somewhere out there."

As I leaned against the cold metal fuselage and peered out of the cabin canopy, I froze!

"Skipper, we're on fire! There's a small hole with flames coming from it."

By now my heart was pounding, because fire in an airplane spells mortal danger.

"Where's the fire?"

"Near the back end of the inner engine."

"Maybe the engine fire extinguisher can douse the flames."

Throttling back the inner engine, Roper then feathered its propeller. This turned its three blades so that their edges pointed straight ahead and the propeller didn't rotate. This allowed the fire extinguisher to be activated.

Following Roper's directions, I pushed the red button which activated the fire extinguisher built into the engine. Tensely I watched to see if the fire would go out. It didn't!

"The fire's getting bigger!" I exclaimed.

If Roper had been able to see the fire for himself, he might have realized the futility of trying to put it out and would have immediately ordered the crew to bail out. As it was, these crucial two or three minutes had been lost!

We were now in deadly peril! Fanned by the 260-mile-per-hour slipstream, the fire was acting like a huge blowtorch, cutting its way through the metal structure of the wing. Any moment disaster could overtake us; the wing might break off or the fuel tank explode!

I grabbed Roper's parachute as a frighteningly loud bang came from the burning wing. The wheel that controlled the ailerons jerked counterclockwise in Roper's hands. Working frantically, I managed to get one side of his parachute clipped on. The wheel jerked further counterclockwise, and loud bangs rapidly followed one another. Roper was off his seat, pulling with all his weight and strength on the wheel in a vain effort to stop it turning.

With each bang, the starboard wing rose higher and higher, while the port dipped ever lower. I realized that the fire had destroyed the aileron controls in the wing, forcing the starboard aileron to swing down and the port aileron to turn up. This forced the plane into a sharp banking dive to port that pressed me tightly against the side of the cabin.

Now, everything moved at lightning speed as the Lancaster flipped upside down and plunged toward Mother Earth some fifteen thousand feet below.

Because of the malfunctioning ailerons, the plane was held in a tight spin; tremendous centrifugal forces crushed me against the fuselage. The vicelike grip of these five or six G's (perhaps even more) held me in a fetal position, unable to lift a hand or raise my chin, which was being pressed painfully against my chest. A cold numbness closed over me as I realized we were all going to die. In two minutes it would be all over. I wondered what—if anything—lay beyond death. Heaven? Hell? Purgatory? Some ethereal, spiritual plane? Nothing? Thoughts of barrack-room arguments over the subject came to my mind. Whatever lay on the other side of death, I would soon experience it!

These icy, benumbing thoughts ended with a rending, roaring explosion of light, noise, and violence; in the split second before oblivion engulfed me, I thought, *We've hit the ground. This is death!*

# BACK FROM THE ABYSS

A large, fuzzy, red ball moved across a void of intense blackness and disappeared, leaving the blackness complete and unrelieved. What could it be? I wondered vaguely. Again the fuzzy ball appeared and passed from view. Then again. But this time it was smaller, less fuzzy, and elongated. As it appeared once more, I snapped back to full consciousness and saw a sharply defined "comet" of fire—D-Donald plunging to earth!

I realized I was falling through a cold, winter night sky. My hand flew to the parachute to pull the ripcord—nothing! There was no ripcord ring! I experienced a moment of sheer panic. Looking down in the moonlight, I breathed a sigh of relief as I realized I had clipped the parachute on as if I were left-handed. Reaching across the parachute, I grabbed the ring and pushed out the ripcord. The chute burst open, the tightly packed white silk blossoming into a glorious canopy of life above me. With a jerk, my free-fall speed of around 150 miles per hour was reduced to something like jumping off a twelve-foot wall.

I continued gazing up at that white silk canopy shining brightly in the moonlight; my heart was filled with thankfulness for the unknown young WAAF parachute packer who had so faithfully and efficiently carried out her life-saving task. I searched the moonlit sky for another parachute. Was it possible Roper had also been blown out of the cockpit? But all I could see was the plume of fire streaking earthward. I watched in fascinated horror at the tragedy being played out before my eyes: D-Donald smashing into the ground with a burst of flame. I felt numb; I knew in my heart that my six friends and comrades-in-arms had just perished.[1]

My parachute swiveled in the air, and I lost sight of the crash site. I now became aware that one of the straps of my parachute harness was cutting into my groin. Pulling on the shroud lines, I assumed a sitting position in a futile attempt to lessen the pressure. While I was struggling with the parachute, I hit the ground painfully, landing on one of the steel rails of a railway track! For several weeks, I would feel the pain from this jarring blow in my lower spine. It was amazing that I didn't break my back.

I sat for a few minutes to recover from the shock of hitting the ground. I looked at my watch; the luminous dial read exactly 1:30 A.M. Some two years later I would learn how significant that time was. Scrambling to my feet, I released the harness and gathered it up with the parachute, looking for a place to hide them. I saw I had landed next to a small copse of trees, an ideal spot. As I ran down the embankment toward the trees, I felt sharp stones jabbing the sole of my left foot. Only then did I realize I had lost my left shoe in the explosion.

Among the trees, I quickly covered my parachute with dead leaves. I had just finished when I heard voices coming my direction. Thinking they were the Germans who had shot down our plane, I wondered desperately how to evade capture.

Then I heard another sound: a train laboring slowly up the incline on which I had landed. Crouching among the trees, I saw it loom out of the darkness as it rounded a curve. I watched tensely as it approached. At the same time the voices were also coming closer. When the engine passed, I saw it was pulling a freight train and that it was traveling slow enough for me to climb aboard.

I climbed up the embankment toward the tracks and, in spite of my shoeless foot, raced alongside the train. When an open-topped wagon slowly began to pass, I made a lunging jump and grasped the top of the wagon. I was swung off my feet, but by using all my strength, I pulled myself up until I could get a foothold. Moments later, I collapsed, panting, on the bales of hay that filled the railway car. When I regained my breath I used my small penknife to remove my insignia from my battledress tunic and threw them from the train. Then I moved the bales of hay around to make a hiding space in the center of the wagon. Wearily I dropped into it and fell fast asleep.

That evening, about five hours earlier, in the old picturesque village of Ickenham, my mother and father had heard the steady drone of hundreds of bombers passing overhead. They wondered whether I was up there in the cold, moonlit, night sky. My mother could not go to bed that evening. She was troubled with a strange, restless anxiety. Finally, she went into my bedroom and lay on my bed, leaving the light on. "O God," she prayed, "if my boy is out there, please keep him safe."

From time to time she glanced at the wall clock. The time passed slowly—12:00 A.M., 1:00 A.M.—but still sleep would not come. Again she whispered that prayer, "O God, if my boy is out there, please keep him safe."

As the hands slowly moved around the clock, her anxiety and restlessness intensified until she cried out aloud, "Dear God, if my boy is out there, please keep him safe." Suddenly peace came over her, and she noticed the clock on the wall with its hands pointing exactly to 1:30 A.M. Then she fell asleep.

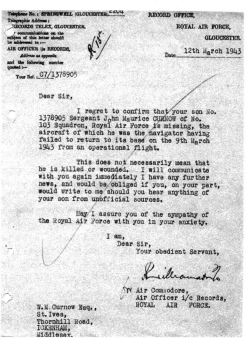

The next morning she related this experience to my father, saying that something bad had happened to me during the night, but that she knew I was all right. Later that day, my parents received a telegram from my squadron informing them I was missing.

When I eventually got back to England in April 1945, my mother told me what she had experienced that night. She then asked, "John, what time was it when you were shot down?"

"One-thirty in the morning," I replied. We just stared at each other!

*RAF letter to my father, confirming that I was missing in action*

Though God had little or no place in my heart at that time, I now know He answered the intercessory prayers of a pleading mother!

Not only did my mother keep all the letters I wrote home, she also kept copies of every letter she wrote to me while I was a POW, numbering them in order to keep track of them. In answer to the first letter I wrote from the POW camp, she wrote in her letter No. 4:

> Oh, John, we know from your words, "I was brought very close to God" that something dreadful had happened, and we longed to know that you were all right. It was a miraculous escape. Everybody marvels who hears of it. If any proof be needed for answered prayer, surely it is here. Always carry it humbly in your heart, John dear, how God in His mercy, kept you safe. If you can only hold steadfastly to that, then you have been given a strength, in His own mysterious way, that will help you through troubles and difficulties. It seems incredible you could have come through such an ordeal unscathed.
>
> Do you remember me describing a very vivid dream I had (long before you joined the service) of watching men parachuting from a plane? I never forgot the feeling of deep conviction that one day a parachute would come to mean much to me personally. The night you "went out" [to Munich] I was very restless, and I couldn't go to bed. Still dressed, I had to lie on your bed, with your dressing gown as a cover, and holding tightly to one of the cuffs. I shall always remember how I prayed to God to watch over you that night if you were "out there."

While my mother slept on my bed and I slept between the bales of hay in that railway wagon, the large clock on the wall of the control tower at Elsham Wolds read 3:15 A.M., telling the personnel that the first returning bomber would be arriving back at any time. Everyone was quiet as they listened expectantly. When the first faint throb of the four Merlin engines was heard, someone took out his wallet and held up a pound note. "A quid on D-Donald!" he challenged. As usual, there were no takers.

As the roar of that first Lancaster grew louder, the loudspeaker came alive: "Hello Bottie. Hello Bottie. Y-Yorker calling. Y-Yorker calling. Requesting permission to pancake. Over."

In stunned silence the tower personnel looked at each other. They knew the last of the old Halifax squadron crews was gone.

I learned the details of what happened in the control tower at Elsham Wolds from my sister Meriel, who heard it through a series of unusual circumstances. She told me the story shortly after I got back to England. When the family learned I had been shot down, Meriel, who was serving at an RAF station in the north of England, took compassionate leave to be with our parents. A week after the tragic event, she was returning to her station, and found herself sitting opposite a young RAF officer on the train. They struck up a conversation, and my sister told him that her brother had recently been shot down.

"Oh, I'm so sorry. What squadron was he in?" he asked.

"The 103rd, at Elsham Wolds."

"Why, that's my squadron," he exclaimed. "What was his name?"

"John Curnow."

"Johnny Roper's navigator. They were our senior crew." He went on to tell my sister that his girlfriend was a WAAF who worked in the control tower there and that she had told him what had taken place that night when, for the first time in months, D-Donald was not the first bomber to arrive back to base.

Meriel asked me, "Was that true, John, you always got back first?"

"Yes, Mel, every time," I replied.

"How on earth did you manage that?" she asked.

As I explained our technique and our reasons, she just shook her head.

---

[1] As I write, the police report of our crash, made the day after the tragedy, has recently been found in the French archives. It states that only one body (the pilot's) was found in the wreckage of the fuselage. It further states that the other five bodies had been ejected from the plane. Wreckage of D-Donald was scattered over a large area. The explosion must have been much more violent than I had supposed. Were those five killed by the explosion? Were they unconscious all the way down? Or were some of them conscious as they plummeted to their deaths? These questions lie heavy on my heart.

# "FOR YOU, THE WAR IS OVER"

I woke to find the train had stopped in a large marshalling yard. Later, I discovered that we were in the city of Reims, only eight miles southwest of where our bomber had crashed. I had slept through the jolting and clanking of the wagons when the train had come to a stop.

Cautiously looking around in the light of early dawn, I saw an iron footbridge spanning the tracks not fifty feet away. Anyone crossing that bridge would be able to see me if he glanced in my direction. Just then, a man started to climb the nearby steps to the bridge. Tensely I waited to see if he would look my way. He didn't. But I knew I had to leave the marshalling yard before it got any lighter.

Dodging from cover to cover, I slipped out of the yard onto a road heading south. After about a mile, this road joined another on the southern edge of the city, beyond which lay open countryside. It was now quite light, and as I hurried westward I noticed that the few Frenchmen I passed looked at me curiously. And well they might, since I was wearing only one shoe and was not dressed for being outdoors on a cold, winter morning. (My navigator's cabin in the Lancaster was heated, so I didn't wear flight gear like the other members of the crew.) Also, I might run into a German patrol at any moment. As quickly as possible I had to find a place to hide until nightfall.

In about half an hour I came to a low bridge over a canal. Crossing the bridge, I ran down some steps to the towpath. Nervously I hurried past a house built next to the canal; its curtains, I was happy to see, were still drawn. As I walked alongside a tall wooden fence, I wondered whether I would be able to hide on the other side. I looked around. Seeing no one, I grabbed the top, pulled myself up, and peered over into a neglected area at the end of the long, back garden of the house. An ideal hiding place. Quickly I dropped into the garden and crawled behind some bushes and lay down. In this position, I was hidden from the house about two hundred feet away. Tensely I waited to see if anyone had seen me. No one came to investigate.

At last I was able to relax and take stock of my situation. I knew I would have to get help from the French, but I also knew that any approach would have to be made in complete secrecy. It was vitally important that a prospective helper be fully assured that no one else had seen me. If the Germans found a Frenchman helping me, I would become a prisoner of war, but the French helper would be summarily executed.

I had been cold ever since being shot down. Now, as I lay in the garden, I was happy to feel the warm rays of the rising sun. But a new discomfort arose. I began to feel hungry, which reminded me of the escape kit in my pocket. Opening the packet, I distributed its contents in various pockets and ate one of the concentrated food tablets. It gave me some needed nourishment, but it did nothing to assuage my hunger.

After a while I dozed off, but was awakened by the whining of a dog! Opening my eyes a little, I slowly moved my head so I could see the dog—a medium-sized mongrel about twenty feet away. I was careful not to make eye contact which might cause it to bark, which, in turn, could prompt someone to come out of the house to investigate. I lay quietly as if asleep. The dog continued to whine and whimper for a minute or so, then went away, much to my relief. But after a while it returned. Again I lay motionless. Again the dog whimpered for a while before withdrawing. This routine continued throughout the day, and I got very little rest. It was a very long day!

As the sun sank toward the horizon, the temperature began to drop. The chill of approaching nightfall, plus the discomfort of lying for hours on the hard, cold ground, called for action. Cautiously and painfully getting to my feet, I peered over the fence. The coast was clear. Without waiting for darkness, I climbed over the fence and headed south along the canal towpath.

Before long the canal took a turn to the southeast, so I left the towpath and cut west across the barren countryside. It was painful walking barefoot on the rough ground. I was relieved when, after about an hour, I came to a road. By then night had fallen, and I was glad the sky was clear and the stars were visible. Locating the North Star, I figured the road was heading due south. I followed it, and when I came to a side road heading west, I turned onto it.

Walking on the roads, I made fairly good progress. But after a few hours my pace began to slow because of the increasing discomfort to my shoeless foot. I began to wonder whether I would be able to continue walking through the night.

About this time I rounded a bend in the road and saw that I was about to enter a village. Seeing no alternative, I cautiously made my way through the village, keeping to the shadows. Nothing stirred; the village was fast asleep.

About two hours later I came to a fork in the road. Taking the road to the right, I soon came to another village which I skirted before reaching a road leading west into a forest. Walking through the trees gave me a sense of safety, as they would offer instant cover if a German patrol came along.

As the hours slowly dragged on, I was reduced to limping along at barely a mile an hour. Every step with my shoeless foot was painful. I knew time was running out for me, and I found myself repeating again and again, "I must get help. I must get help." Hunger, cold, lack of sleep, and my shoeless foot all combined to plunge my morale to rock bottom!

At last the road emerged from the forest, and a short time later I saw an isolated house set back a little from the road. This was what I needed—a house all by itself. With a faint glimmer of hope I opened the gate and knocked loudly on the door. I waited a short while and then banged louder. A few moments later a light streamed out of an upstairs window, lighting a patch of ground behind me. I stepped back into the light so I could be seen.

After a short while, the door opened, but my hopes were dashed. Standing in the doorway was a burley man with his right hand raised above his head—holding a long knife that glinted

*The isolated house near the village of Nanteuil-la-Foret to which I crawled seeking help.*

in the light behind him. Pleadingly I said, "English. Royal Air Force. Flyer. Airplane." He started shouting at me, and the hand that held the knife began jerking up and down. He took a threatening step toward me. With a heavy heart I turned and limped back to the road.

Dejectedly I continued walking. About an hour later, as the dawn of a new day began to lighten the sky, I sat down by the roadside. Another forest lay about a quarter of a mile to the left. Nearer was a lone house, set back from the road, beyond which the road curved right to a small village.

Leaving the road and keeping my eyes open for anyone who might be about that early in the morning, I crept toward the house. I knew someone from the village might see me, but by now I was physically and emotionally at the end of my tether. I didn't really care anymore.

I was lying in a slight depression near the house, pondering my next move, when a woman came out of the house. Softly I called out, "English. RAF."

Startled, she looked in my direction, and I made myself visible to her. She scurried back inside the house, and I waited, imagining how she and her husband were discussing the crisis I had so abruptly brought into their lives. They had to make a life or death decision.

*The mayor's house in Nanteuil-la-Foret from which I escaped—briefly!*

Could they be certain I had not been seen by some quisling[1] looking their way from the village?

After a few minutes her husband emerged and came toward me smiling. The way he approached me openly in daylight, I knew the game was up. If he had been planning to help me, he would have given a quick glance in my direction and then headed toward the nearby forest. As it was, he beckoned me to follow him. Making a dash for the forest was out of the question in my weakened condition. So with a feeling of resignation, I followed the man into the village. I had no anger toward him. I knew I had approached his house too openly.

He led me to the mayor's house and knocked on the door. A kindly looking man opened it. My escort spoke to him rapidly in French which, of course, I couldn't understand. As the mayor beckoned us in, his wife joined him. They both looked sympathetically at me. I pointed to my shoeless foot. The woman nodded and disappeared. A few minutes later she returned carrying an old left shoe. It was a little tight, but my foot was swollen; otherwise it fit perfectly. When I put it on and tied the lace, my morale rocketed from ground zero!

As they led me into a back room with a solitary couch, I indicated to them that I was hungry. The woman again smiled and left the room, returning shortly with a plate of food and a glass of wine. After watching me ravenously devour the food, they pointed to the couch, saying I should sleep, and left the room.

## "FOR YOU, THE WAR IS OVER"

I awoke with a start and sat up. I don't know how long I was asleep, but sitting on a chair in the doorway was a French policeman, a gendarme. Tapping the pistol in his holster, he told me in broken English that I was a prisoner and that the German army field police were on their way to pick me up.

I lay back down on the coach with a feeling of resignation. But as I did so, I noticed that the window behind the couch was wide open! I couldn't believe the gendarme would allow security to be so lax! I pretended to go back to sleep, but looking through slitted eyes I saw someone hand him a glass of wine and a plate of food. While his attention was diverted, I sprang over the back of the couch and jumped out of the window. Only as I was going out the window did I see that the house was built on a slope and that I was jumping not from the ground level, but from the second floor! I hit the ground a little heavily, but wasn't hurt. Picking myself up, I took off running, happy that I now had a shoe on each foot.

I got a good start on the gendarme. He was much older than I, maybe in his late forties; he didn't follow me through the window, but instead, ran down the stairs leading to the back door. After several seconds I heard the crack of his pistol. Glancing quickly over my shoulder, I saw him a long way back, firing his revolver as he ran. I knew he had little chance of hitting me at that range, but I zigzagged until I counted six shots. His pistol was empty. I soon outran him, losing him behind some houses.

I had reached the road leading back into the forest when my luck ran out. The mayor's son blocked my way, holding a large dagger in his raised hand. When I had jumped out of the window, he had run out the front door to cut me off.

Panting heavily, I stood facing this scared but determined young man, pondering how best to tackle him. But before I could regain my breath, a military car sped around the bend in the road. The young man waved his arms and shouted excitedly in German; the car came to an abrupt halt. For the first time in my life I found myself looking, at close range, into the muzzle of a pistol held by an enemy quite prepared to squeeze the trigger. Still panting and with pounding heart, I slowly raised my hands above my head. Three

German soldiers jumped out of the car. One frisked me and then said in fairly good English, "You are a prisoner of war. For you the war is over!"

If I had awakened five minutes earlier, I would have been able to reach the forest. I had learned in combat training how to deal with someone armed only with a knife. As it was, I found myself sitting beside an armed German soldier while the car sped back to Reims.

The way the Germans drove through the villages, forcing the French people to hurriedly get out of their way, showed the arrogance of the occupying forces. This made me feel uneasy about how I would be treated.

*Note: As I write, I have before me a copy of the police report of my capture, recently found in the French archives. It identifies the village in which I was captured as Nanteuil-la-Foret. From this report I have been able to retrace the route I took when leaving Reims. I have also been able to identify the village I passed through and, I believe, the roadside house where I tried to get help. The report also gives the names of the French people involved in my capture.*

---

[1] A traitor who collaborates with the occupying forces of the enemy.

# A SMALL BIBLE AND A LARGE RADIATOR

Arrival at the military prison forcefully reminded me that my life had undergone a dramatic change and that I was no longer a free person. There had been necessary restrictions in the Air Force, but I had still been free. Now, as I sat on the edge of the plain wooden bunk in the small, cold, prison cell, I understood with a sense of grim finality what it means to be "deprived of one's freedom"—to be a prisoner at the mercy of a ruthless enemy.

I had been frisked and pushed into a cell. The heavy door slammed shut behind me and I heard the key turn in the lock. For a few minutes I struggled with discouragement. Then I realized that although I had been frisked, I had not been thoroughly searched and I still had my escape kit. Taking the different items from various pockets, I started to hide them. I put the six-inch hacksaw blade inside my right sock so that I was standing on it. I believed that even in a thorough search I would not be asked to remove my socks. Taking off my trousers, I cut a few stitches at the bottom of the cuffs and inserted the small compass.

The bigger, and more important, task was to hide the three silk maps of Europe. The only place I felt I could successfully hide them was in the lining of the waistband of my trousers. I cut some of the lining stitches, making an inconspicuous opening about an inch and a half long. Folding the maps into long, narrow strips, I fed them, one by one, through the opening until they were evenly distributed around the waistband.

## SHOT DOWN!

At first I thought I would hide the German and French paper money in the lining of my jacket, but because they made a crackling noise, I decided to leave them in a pocket. I didn't want to draw attention to the other items I had hidden.

I had barely completed this work when the key rattled in the lock, and the door swung open. The guard told me to take off my uniform and shoes, which he took away. After a short while these were returned to me. As soon as the guard had left, I anxiously examined my trousers. The money and my penknife were gone, but the maps were still there. In spite of several searches, the Germans never found those maps. The compass, also, was still where I had hidden it.

Later in the morning the guard returned and motioned me to follow him. Everything was new to me, of course, and I didn't know what to expect so my heart beat faster every time I came face to face with a German. After all, Germans were the evil enemy that was ravaging Europe.

From the cellblock I was marched across a small courtyard and into another building. At the door of the Kommandant's office my guard knocked sharply and opened the door. Pushing me inside, he saluted smartly and said, "Heil Hitler!" The mere mention of that name sent a shiver down my spine. Though I had studied German at school for three years, I wasn't able to understand what the guard said as he spoke briefly to the Kommandant.

Regarding me with not unfriendly eyes, the officer beckoned me forward. Coming to attention, I clicked my heels in salute and took two or three steps toward his desk. As I did so I was surprised to see, spread before him, one of my own maps from my plane, showing a red line I had drawn from Elsham Wolds. I steeled myself as I quickly looked at the officer, hoping I had not shown any sign of recognition.

"Who are you?" he asked in perfect English.

"Royal Air Force. Sergeant John Curnow, 1378905," I replied, not knowing I had already been commissioned as pilot officer with the new service number of 142321.

After writing down this information, he demanded "What squadron are you from?"

"Sir, international law requires me to give only my name, number, and rank. I can give no other information," I replied, my heart beating faster.

Tapping the map, he said, "Look, Curnow, we already know you are from the 103rd Squadron, based at Elsham Wolds, so you may as well admit it." I remained silent, looking stonily ahead.

After a slight pause, he continued, "You are a very lucky airman." I steeled myself for what I knew he was going to say next. Looking into my eyes, he continued in a soft, low, yet challenging, voice, "The other six members of your crew are all dead." He searched my face for some sign of a reaction, but I believe he found none. I also believe he was not sure I was the missing crew member of the ill-fated D-Donald. Seeing he wasn't going to get any further information from me, he terminated the interrogation, and the guard took me back to my cell.

By midday I was again feeling the gnawing pangs of hunger. Except for the small amount of food the French family had given me, I hadn't eaten for nearly two days. I was relieved when the cell door was opened and the guard said, *"Essen,"* as he plunked down on the small table a tray of food—two thick slices of rye bread, some sausage, a pat of margarine (that tasted like cream), and a mug of steaming hot ersatz coffee. It all looked very appetizing to my hungry eyes! *At least they aren't going to let me starve,* I thought, as I ravenously attacked the food.

With my hunger assuaged, I lay on the wooden bunk on a thin straw-filled mattress, called a *palliasse,* and fell fast asleep. I awakened only when the guard brought me an evening meal, much the same as lunch. After two meals and some time to sleep, I felt I was returning to normal.

The next morning when I awoke, I wondered for a moment where I was. I shivered, not so much from cold (though it was cold in the unheated cell) as from the realization that I had just spent my first night in captivity. I had never experienced solitary confinement before, and as I sat on the edge of the hard bunk, staring miserably at the blank walls, I pondered what lay ahead.

After a breakfast of more rye bread, I again heard the sound of a key turning in the lock. As the door swung open, I saw, standing beside the guard, two men in blue-gray uniforms. I was unfamiliar with German uniforms, and a flash of fear went through me as the thought entered my mind that these might be Gestapo agents. But they quickly informed me that I was being handed over to the *Luftwaffe,* the German Air Force. The *Luftwaffe* uniform would become very familiar to me in the days and months to come.

The Luftwaffe guards marched me from the military prison to the nearby railway station. And so began my journey into Germany.

While one of the guards went inside the station, the other guard and I waited out on the street. French pedestrians gave quick, furtive glances in my direction as they went about their business. However, I noticed one Frenchman standing some distance away looking at me sympathetically. I wondered whether he belonged to the French Underground Resistance. When my guard turned in his direction, he hurried away. The occupation of their country by German invaders was a grim experience for the French, as it was for the citizens of all the other occupied countries of Europe. As I saw how the people lived in constant fear, I knew that the war we were fighting was totally justified and that the terrible Nazi evil that had engulfed almost all of Europe had to be destroyed.

While we waited for the other guard to return, the guard who had stayed with me asked in fairly good English, "Why English and Germans fighting each other? We are *bruders* (brothers)." Looking around furtively, he leaned toward me and whispered, "We should be fighting together against the French!" He didn't speak to me again.

When the other guard returned, they escorted me to a train at one of the platforms. The Germans ordered some French passengers to vacate a compartment, and with looks of resignation, mingled with bitterness, they hastily complied. I sat in silence as we traveled to Brussels, Belgium, where we changed to another train bound for Cologne, Germany. The guards again commandeered a compartment. My lips tightened when the train stopped at Aachen and I knew I was inside Germany, the country we had bombed so many times.

# A SMALL BIBLE AND A LARGE RADIATOR

At Cologne, the guards took me to a basement area under the railway station. Now that I was no longer in control of my life, I had become strangely resigned to whatever lay ahead. I watched, with fascination and disgust, dozens of huge cockroaches scurrying around the cold, damp floor. The only other time I had seen these loathsome insects was in the biology laboratory at school where we had dissected them to study their alimentary canal and other organs. How far off those schooldays now seemed! Yet it had been barely three years. How quickly the war had changed me from a carefree teenager to a man fighting for the freedom of his beloved country and that of Europe.

Soon I was on another train heading south, gazing out the window at the incredibly scenic Rhine Valley. But I was in no mood to enjoy the beauty of that great river with its ancient castles perched on the hillsides. I would have to wait for a vacation with my family many years later for that pleasure. However, in my first letter home I did refer to this beauty, and in her letter No. 2 to me, my mother replied, "Yes, the country that now holds you is lovely. Beauty knows no frontiers. When all men come to love her glories for themselves, no matter within what borders, the world will be so much happier."

Leaving the Rhine Valley, the train finally arrived at Frankfurt. There we transferred to a military automobile and headed into the countryside.

After traveling for about half an hour at high speed, the car screeched to a stop outside a large isolated building in a wooded area. *Why do the Germans always drive so fast?* I wondered. *Maybe it was the blitzkrieg mentality that had worked so well for their army!* I had arrived at Dulag Luft, the *Luftwaffe's* interrogation center for captured airmen. I was taken to a small cell, measuring about six by ten feet, which was to be my "home" for the next thirteen days. The only furniture was a wooden bunk with a thin *palliasse* and two army blankets, a small table, and a stool. In the wall opposite the door was a window with thick frosted glass which allowed light in, but through which I could see nothing. Presumably there were bars on the outside. Below the window was a very large radiator. I wondered why such a small room needed such a large radiator.

Adding to that mystery was the fact that, in spite of it being winter, it was not in use. The mystery would be resolved a few nights later.

I had barely taken stock of my new surroundings, when the door opened and an English-speaking officer told me to strip down to my underwear. He wanted all my clothes for another inspection. I asked whether he wanted my socks as well. Waving his hand, he let me keep them on. I still had my hacksaw blade! But I was upset when he told me my navigator's watch would be confiscated because it was British government property, not mine personally. This really annoyed me because if I had been warned about this back in England I could easily have hidden it somewhere in the cell. From then on I could not keep track of the time.

Wrapping a blanket around me to keep warm, I waited for at least half an hour for my clothes to be returned. I felt sure that this time, with such a lengthy search, my maps and compass would be found. Gleefully, when I had my clothes once more, I found the maps and compass still where I had hidden them. Psychologically, this small victory over the Germans gave a big boost to my morale. For me the war was *not* over!

The next day I received a visit by a smiling middle-aged man dressed in civilian clothes. He had charming manners and introduced himself as a representative of the International Red Cross (IRC) in Switzerland, whose responsibility it was to look after the interests of prisoners of war. First he commiserated with my being a POW and told me that he would see that my parents quickly learned that I was safe. However, to do this he would need some personal information. He started by asking who my parents were and where they lived.

Back in England we had been warned about German intelligence officers posing as IRC representatives. We were told that genuine representatives did not interview prisoners at this interrogation center. I challenged him, telling him bluntly that he was bogus and was no more an IRC representative than I was. He tried to persuade me that I was making a mistake, but finally realizing I had called his bluff, he withdrew.

# A SMALL BIBLE AND A LARGE RADIATOR

For the next few days a uniformed officer continued to interrogate me, at which times I doggedly stuck to name, number, and rank only. I was once more visited by a man dressed in civilian clothes. While admitting that the first "civilian" was not a genuine IRC representative, he claimed that he was, and produced valid-looking documents as proof. When I told him that his identification documents were fakes like himself, he left. After this I stopped receiving further visits. Now the German tactics were about to change and the radiator mystery would be solved, as I would learn that night.

Turning in for the night, I wrapped myself in the two blankets to keep warm. Sometime later I awoke, drenched in perspiration. The large radiator was so hot I couldn't touch it, and the cell was like an oven. I banged on the door, but to no avail. The Germans were now resorting to torture tactics. Stripping down to just my underwear, I finally dropped off into a fitful sleep. Hours later I again woke up, but this time I was shivering with cold. The radiator had been turned off, and the outside early morning chill of mid-March had dramatically lowered the inside temperature. Wearily I got dressed again and, wrapped in my blankets, fell asleep.

This psychological and physical torture continued night after night, worsening the mental stress and boredom of my total isolation. The only relief came when my meals arrived or when I had to visit the bathroom. One day I asked one of the more sympathetic guards whether I could have something to read. He brought me a small King James Bible.

In spite of not being religious, I spent hours poring over that Bible. As I read about Jesus, a strange peace relieved the mental and emotional stress I was experiencing. My mind went back to my early childhood when my sister Barbara would read stories to me from *Uncle Arthur's Bedtime Stories.*[1] From those stories I had learned how Jesus loved little children and how He answered their prayers. However, my childhood interest in spiritual things had not lasted. When I was about eight or nine years old the "Blue Laws" in England were relaxed, and shops which sold newspapers, tobacco products, and candy, were allowed to open on Sunday. One Sunday, my sister and I succumbed to temptation. We played truant from Sunday School and spent our penny offerings on candy. We never went back to Sunday School. Now, ten or eleven years later, in that cold cell, I found myself being drawn back to the Jesus of my early childhood.

But the nightly hot and cold torture was wearing me down. On the morning of the thirteenth day, when I again was grilled for information, I was so mentally and physically exhausted, I gave in. I admitted I was the missing crew member of D-Donald. This satisfied the Teutonic mind which needed confirmation of what my captors were already sure of.

That night the radiator was not turned on. For the first time in over a week I slept soundly and wasn't awakened in the middle of the night, bathed in a pool of perspiration. The next day I was released into the small, adjacent transit camp.[2] I was sorry I had to leave the Bible behind.

---

[1] Each year my mother would purchase a copy of the latest edition of the *Bedtime Stories* from Newbold College students who called at our house. Young men trained at this college for the ministry in the Seventh-day Adventist Church.

[2] New POWs were kept in this camp until there was a big enough group to transfer to a permanent camp.

# MIDNIGHT MADNESS

In the transit camp I was relieved and thankful to see other men dressed in the blue uniform of the Royal Air Force. I quickly forgot my dejection over losing the drawn-out struggle with the Germans. The nightmare of the past two weeks was over, and once again I was among my fellow countrymen. There were about twenty POWs in the camp, and I spent much of the day swapping experiences with a number of them.

The next day, March 27, 1943, I wrote my first letter home as a kriegie,[1] using one of two special POW letter forms the Germans had given me. I am surprised sixty-one years later at how stoical I was as I wrote that letter:

It has been a very long time since I last wrote a letter. Little did I know when I wrote that last letter that the next one would be written from inside a German prison camp. At first it was a bit of a shock, but I am settling down to it, but not so much as to forget that the freedom of England, for an Englishman, is a thousand times better than the privations of an enemy prison camp. One thing that will help me considerably is that you at home do not worry as to my comforts and welfare, for they are better than you would expect. The food here in the camp is excellent. And the other things that go to make up a civilized and interesting daily life are also of a high standard.

It may sound strange, but in a few ways this has done me good, that otherwise would not have been done. One, which is by far the most important (that is, in fact, the most important thing in life), is that it has brought me into contact with God, into a relationship with Him that before never existed, I am sorry to say.

Unfortunately, I found no encouragement in POW camp life to help me maintain this connection with God. Also, I never received the early letters of encouragement my godly mother wrote me. It wasn't very long before I forgot about God and drifted back into my old secular way of life.

Among the letters from this time that my daughter, Dr. Sally Mashburn, sorted for me are handwritten copies of fifty-six of my mother's letters, most of which I never received. In addition, there are seventeen letters returned to my mother as undeliverable. In her second letter (which I didn't receive) my mother wrote, "God bless you. Hold fast to your need of Him in your life. You *will* discover its value."

Two days later I wrote my second letter in which I said,

The weather here is perfect, a cloudless blue sky with a warm sun and a gentle breeze, with pleasant landscapes to gaze upon, spoiled only by the barbed wire fence surrounding the camp. I, being an Englishman in the hands of the enemy, have but one thought, and you being English folk, will, I think, know what it is. Will you occasionally offer up a prayer that someday that thought will become a reality, and with strength of mind and body I will carry it out with success.

My "one thought" was to escape. Of course, the German censorship prevented me saying so outright. I hoped my parents would understand what I was referring to.

Later that same day, as I stood outside the barracks, soaking in the afternoon sunshine, I was approached by a pilot of somewhat unusual appearance. He was tall and slightly stooped. But it was his face and head which drew one's attention. He had a large, hooked nose and bulging eyes that peered at you with an intense, penetrating look. His dark hair grew only on the sides and back of his head, accentuated a high bald dome. Later, I would see him invariably wearing a soft woolen head cover, reminiscent of an old-fashioned nightcap.

After introducing himself as Jack Mason, he abruptly asked whether I was interested in escaping.

"Sure," I replied. "I've escaped once already. But how can you get out of this place?"

"Over the fence; it's only one way. We aren't here long enough to dig a tunnel."

"Climb over the fence! Are you crazy? Not me. I don't want to hang spread-eagled on that fence, riddled with bullets! Ask one of the other chaps."

"I've already asked them, but like you, they all think it would be madness to try to climb over the fence.[2] But believe me, I'm not that daft. Listen to my plan." Looking around furtively, Jack nodded toward the guard box at the corner of the compound.

"See the pillbox under the guard box?[3] That's the place to get out. Because of that pillbox, we only need to climb the inside fence and then we'd be on top of the pillbox, under the floor of the guard box," Mason explained.

*Climb the fence right under the guard box!* I could hardly believe what I was hearing. "Jack, those guard boxes aren't closed-in rooms; they're wide open. The guards would be standing only three or four feet away from us and would certainly hear us climbing the fence."

"Do you think I haven't thought of that?" Jack replied a little impatiently. "The guards won't hear us because every night the wind picks up and makes a dickens of a noise as it blows through all those trees." He nodded toward the trees that surrounded the camp. I had noticed that it got quite noisy before going to bed.

"What about that coil of barbed wire we would have to get over first?"

"I've got that worked out, too. We'll wrap a wardrobe door in a blanket and use that to span the wire."

"Jack, you've obviously put a lot of thought into your plan, but I still see a major problem. They switch the lights on and off."

"Listen, John. I've been here over a week, and I've been watching the guards. The ones that come on duty at midnight are very methodical. They turn on the lights for thirty seconds and then turn them off for exactly two-and-a-half minutes. They stick rigidly to this three-minute routine, bless their Teutonic minds. Two-and-a-half minutes will be enough time for us to get out. What do you think?"

I had to admit Mason wasn't as crazy as I had thought at first. He had everything worked out.

I looked at the tall barbed wire fence with the guards patrolling outside, their rifles slung across their backs. Again I glanced at the guard box, standing stark and menacingly in the corner. I couldn't overlook the obvious risks. But then, the very audacity of the plan appealed to me and made me feel we could pull it off.

"OK, Jack. Count me in!"

The expectant look on his face gave way to a broad smile. We shook hands as we walked back to our barracks.

After the evening meal, the hours dragged. My mind raced with the thoughts of what Mason and I were planning to do. The other chaps considered us crazy to attempt such an escape, and from a rational standpoint they might have been right. But then, what escape-minded kriegie was governed purely by rationality? But we believed the escape plan to be feasible and the calculated risks worth taking. We were daring, but not stupid.

Mason and I again went over the plans. With only two-and-a-half minutes, our success would depend on us acting with precision.

Since there was no floodlight opposite our barracks, much of the space between it and the adjacent barracks remained in the shadows when the lights were turned on. Our plan was to climb out of the window just after the lights were turned off, and then lie in the shaded area until they came on again. Then, the moment the lights were again turned off, we would run for the corner.

As the evening hours slowly passed, I became drowsy and dozed off. I awoke with a start as Mason gently shook me. "It's nearly midnight," he whispered. "Let's see if those guards will come on duty."

Mason was looking at the luminous dial of his watch. (How I missed my navigator's watch the Germans had confiscated!) "It's midnight," he whispered. Tensely we waited to see if the lights would follow the pattern of these particular guards. Only the heavy breathing of some of the men broke the silence. The lights came on and, checking his watch, Jack counted the seconds. "Twenty-seven. Twenty-eight. Twenty-nine. Thirty." The lights went out. "It's them," Mason whispered triumphantly. "I bet the lights will come back on in two-and-a-half minutes."

He continued looking at his watch, and, sure enough, exactly on time the lights were turned on again. Jack gave the thumbs-up sign, and whispered, "Ready?"

Breathing heavily, I nodded my head. There was no backing down now!

As soon as the lights were turned off again, Mason opened the window. The loud sound of wind in the trees greeted our ears. "See what I meant about the noise," Mason whispered as he climbed out of the window. Passing the blanket-covered door to him, I followed, quietly closing the window behind me. No words were spoken as we lay waiting on the cold ground. Since it was his plan, we had agreed that Mason would go first, carrying all the food. That way, none would be lost if I didn't make it.

The lights came on, and I started counting the seconds as we hugged the ground in the darkened area. On time, the lights went out, and Jack whispered, "Now!" With him holding one end of the door and me the other, we raced to the corner of the compound.

*Sketch of my escape plan from Dulag Luft. I was successful; Jack Mason was not.*

With considerable consternation we saw we had made a serious miscalculation! Because the coil of wire curved in the corner, it took up a wider space than we had planned, and the door didn't reach all the way across it to the fence.

With no time to waste, Mason grasped the side of the door firmly with both hands, and urgently whispered, "Go! Go!" He was able to hold the teetering door steady enough for me to crawl over it to the fence. Any noise it made on the loose wire was drowned out by the noise of the wind in the trees.

Seconds later, with my heart pounding, I lay panting on the roof of the pillbox. No sound came from the two guards, except the shuffling of their feet on the wooden floor above me.

Mason tried to crawl across the door, but with no one to hold it steady, it made a terrible noise as it rocked and swayed on the wire. I held my breath.

Suddenly the lights came on, and one of the guards shouted, *"Achtung!"* Looking back over my shoulder, I saw Mason jump back and stretch his arms straight up above his head. "Don't shoot him!" I whispered to myself. Later he told me how thankful he was that the guards had not opened fire.

The guards were now blowing their whistles, indicating there was an attempted escape. What should I do? Soon reinforcements with dogs would arrive. I had to act quickly. Wriggling to the outer edge of the pillbox, I dropped to the ground.

My breath was coming in short, rapid gasps as I stood with my back to the wall of the pillbox, looking at the fully lighted road leading toward the woods. The floodlit area extended about a hundred yards from the compound. For a brief moment I wondered whether I should surrender. But taking the chance that the attention of all the guards was still focused on Mason, I raced, zigzagging, down the road. Hitting me with a rifle shot would be difficult. No shot was fired.

As soon as I reached the forest I dived into the trees and the welcoming darkness. Cautiously I made my way deeper into the forest. After a few minutes I stopped to rest against a tree. Slowly my heart and my breathing returned to normal; the tension of the last six or seven minutes gave way to exhilaration as I realized I had escaped. The freedom I now had was worth the risks I had taken, even if it lasted for only a short time.

I thought of Mason and was sorry he was not there with me. My brief experience in France had taught me it would be harder to make it on my own than if I had a companion. Then I realized with dismay that I had no food supply; it was all with Jack Mason! My spirits fell, for I knew that without food my escape would be short-lived.

But I couldn't just sit there, feeling sorry for myself. It was time to move on. Already the Germans might have discovered that a prisoner was missing and would be organizing search parties. I had to put as much distance as I could between myself and the prison camp before daylight came.

Taking my bearings from the moon showing through the trees, I headed in a general southwesterly direction. Fortunately there was little undergrowth, but even with the moonlight filtering through the trees, it was still slow going.

After an hour or two (it was hard to judge the passing of time without a watch), the moon sank slowly westward. I knew I had to stop. Without the moon to guide me I could wander in circles in the forest. The few stars I could see wouldn't help me keep a straight path. Then I noticed that the trees were thinning out; soon open country lay ahead. Now that I could see the whole sky, I was quickly able to find the Big Dipper constellation, which led me to the North Star. Keeping this star over my right shoulder, I made rapid progress.

As the eastern sky lightened, I found myself skirting a small hill. Just below the summit were numerous large bushes. I slowly climbed the hillside and, being very tired, I flopped down behind one of the bushes and fell into a deep sleep.

The gentle warmth of the afternoon sun awakened me. For a moment I wondered where I was as I lay drowsily enjoying the tranquility of my peaceful surroundings. But any tendency to daydream ended abruptly as I remembered I was a fugitive on the run from my German captors!

Cautiously I peered around. Farmland, awaiting spring cultivation, stretched away to the south and west. I could see no sign of human habitation, but I was happy, nonetheless, for the cover the trees and bushes afforded.

Then my hunger claimed my attention and reminded me that I hadn't eaten for nearly twenty-four hours. Sadly, I thought of the concentrated food Mason had in his pockets. I wondered what chances I would have of finding food in such hostile environs.

Ignoring my hunger, I turned to planning my escape route. Pulling the silk map of Germany from the waistband of my trousers, I spread it on the ground. Thinking of the car journey, I estimated that Dulag Luft was about twenty-five miles west of Frankfurt. As I studied the map, I saw that the city of Mainz would be the ideal place to cross the Rhine River. It was only about twelve miles to the southwest.

My excitement grew as I realized that unoccupied Vichy, France, lay only about sixty-five miles to the south and southwest of Mainz. I decided that this would be my first goal. If I could make it into Vichy, France, I believed I would have a good chance of getting the help I would need to reach my second goal—neutral Switzerland.

As I continued to study my map, I saw that the city of Wiesbaden was about six miles west of where I was, with a highway running south to Mainz. Since this road would have a bridge over the Rhine, I decided to cut southwest across the farmland until I met this highway.

Having determined my immediate route, I again lay down and fell asleep.

---

[1] This was the nickname we prisoners gave ourselves, derived from *Kriegsgefangener,* the German word for prisoner of war.

[2] The fence at Dulag Luft was typical for POW camps, consisting of two barbed wire fences about eight feet high and four feet apart. The space between the fences was filled with loose coils of barbed wire. Inside the camp was another coil of barbed wire at the base of the inner fence.

[3] Dulag Luft was the only camp where I saw concrete pillboxes under the standard wooden guard boxes.

# A BICYCLE AND A VINEYARD

I awoke feeling the chill of on-setting night. The sun was already low on the western horizon, soon it would be dark. As a fugitive in enemy territory, I was now a creature of the night.

I didn't want to reach Mainz before the city was fast asleep, so I walked at a slow, leisurely pace, using the setting sun to keep me heading southwest. I planned to cover the twelve miles in about five hours, stopping occasionally for rests.

After what I estimated to be at least two hours (how I missed having a watch!) I came to the Wiesbaden-Mainz highway and turned south. From then on the going was much easier, but the danger of being detected was also much greater. I was constantly on the alert for the sound of an approaching military or police vehicle. (Wartime demands on gasoline precluded civilian usage in Germany, just as it did in England.) I was always ready to run from the road and lie down so I would not be seen in the headlights.

But all was quiet, and I had the road to myself as the miles slowly slipped behind me. After maybe another two hours, I heard a faint sound ahead. With my heart thumping, I sprang off the road and ran some twenty paces before throwing myself flat on the ground. Tensely I waited, but the sound didn't grow louder. I strained my ears and realized that the sound was the soft, gentle murmuring of the Rhine River.

I resumed walking, and the low murmuring grew louder until I knew the bridge must lie just ahead in the darkness. In England, all important bridges were guarded day and night against possible sabotage by enemy agents. *Do the Germans guard their bridges?* I wondered.

Alert for the slightest sound of human presence, I inched my way forward until suddenly the stone pillars at the end of the bridge loomed out of the darkness ahead.

I left the road. With my heart beating faster and hardly daring to breathe, I crept stealthily toward the bridge, expecting any moment to hear, *"Halt! Wer geht da?"* ("Halt! Who goes there?") After what seemed eternity, I reached the bridge. There was no sign of a guard.

Hugging the stonework, I started across the bridge. Silently I slipped from one shadow to the next, pausing each time to listen. There might be guards at the city end of the bridge, I reasoned. All remained quiet, except for the sound of the water below, the thumping of my heart, and my heavy breathing. I felt sure, that if there were a guard, he would hear all three!

At last I came to the end of the bridge. There was no guard! Mainz was asleep. I stood in the shadow of one of the pillars, waiting for my heart to settle down.

As I looked down the road into the city, I saw it was blocked with a large pile of rubble. The jagged outlines of bombed buildings on either side of the street were starkly silhouetted against the soft light of the moon. For the first time I was personally seeing the havoc caused by our bombing. I felt no remorse, only satisfaction, that Bomber Command had successfully been at work. I felt satisfaction that Nazi Germany was being paid back for all the horror its great evil had brought to London, Coventry, Warsaw, and scores of other cities spread across Europe.

The road to the west along the river also showed signs of damage, so when my heartbeat returned to normal, I crossed the road and headed east. I hugged the buildings so I could quickly take cover in the shadow of a doorway, should a patrol come along.

I passed two or three other roads that were also blocked with rubble. Obviously the bombers had caused extensive damage to the city. Finally I came to a road heading south that was not blocked. Turning down this road, I increased my pace at the expense of caution. I wanted to get out of the city as quickly as possible. I hoped my luck would continue and I wouldn't run into a police patrol.

As I walked through Mainz I lost count of time. Eventually I came to the southern edge of the city. The road curved to the west and joined a country road leading south through farmland. I was happy I had found a minor road to travel. I didn't want to be on the main highway to Bad Kreuznach, a large town to the southwest.

Several miles south of Mainz I came around a bend in the road and saw I was about to enter a large village. Seeing no alternate route, I cautiously approached the village, moving quickly from one shadowy area to another. Soon the road led into an open square with buildings on all four sides. My first thought was to skirt around the edge of the square, staying close to the buildings. Then I decided it would be quicker to first run to a large monument in the center of the square, and then, after checking that all was clear, to run from the square.

However, as I began hurrying toward the monument, some dogs started barking. Just as I reached the monument, several floodlights came on, lighting the whole square. Fortunately they were on a building on the far side of the square, which left me in the shadow of the monument. Though I was in the only unlit spot in the whole square, I felt I was standing in broad daylight as those probing eyes searched every nook and cranny. With bated breath I stood motionless, trying to melt into the very stone of the monument.

After several minutes the dogs quieted down, but the lights remained on. I wondered if they would stay on for the rest of the night. But then, as abruptly as they had come on, they were turned off. I waited a short while, in case the lights should come back on. Then slipping away from the protection of the monument, I ran from the square and out of the village.

As the night dragged on, I found myself walking almost automatically. How different it would have been had Jack Mason been walking beside me. At times I felt discouraged as hunger pangs reminded me I couldn't go indefinitely without food. Thirst, too, was adding to my discomfort. It had been more than thirty hours since I had had a drink. But then I would remind myself that Vichy, France, was now less than sixty miles away. The thought would add a little zest to my stride.

Once again the eastern sky began to lighten, and soon daylight spread across the countryside. Anxiously I looked around, but the flat, uncultivated farmland offered no cover, not even a bush to hide behind. With nowhere to hide I kept walking, hoping that no vehicle would come along.

After some time, I saw a small pile of hay close to the roadside. It didn't look very promising, but any hiding place was better than nothing. Besides, I had been walking all night and was very tired. Burrowing into the hay, and making sure I was well covered, I fell asleep.

I was awakened by an itching sensation. Hay had worked its way inside my clothes and was making me itch. Making sure no one was around, I crawled out of my hiding place and brushed myself down.

I wondered what to do next. Hunger and thirst cried out for relief. It was now nearly forty-eight hours since I had eaten or drunk anything. With barren farmland stretching away in every direction, my situation looked hopeless. Then I noticed, on the far side of a field, a mound that raised my hopes. It looked like the kind of place in which farmers in England stored potatoes and other root crops through the winter.

Hurrying across the field, I clawed a hole in the hard dirt with my bare hands. With keen anticipation I probed in through a layer of straw. Disappointed, I felt something large and round. It was not potatoes as I had hoped. But, still, it was food, and I was ready to eat anything. Pulling one out, I saw it was some kind of beet. Brushing off some dirt, I sank my teeth into it. As I started to chew a mouthful, it began to burn my mouth and throat. Quickly I spat it out, but too late. The burning sensation continued, and left me with a terrible thirst. The "beet" was most likely a *mangelwurzel,* used only as cattle fodder.

Never before had I felt so miserable as I did at that moment. The burning sensation passed fairly quickly, but the intense thirst lasted for hours.

Realizing it would be futile to return to the pile of hay, I continued my trek to freedom. As the miles slowly dropped behind me, strangely, my pangs of hunger began to slowly subside, leaving in their place a bearable dull ache. But at the same time I became weaker, and my feet heavier.

As I continued walking, I saw I was approaching three houses where the road took a turn to the right.

*What do I do now?* I wondered. To turn back would arouse suspicion if anyone happened to look my way. But to continue presented the risk of being confronted. In Germany, where every young man was in uniform, my youth would demand an explanation. I decided I had no alternative but to keep walking.

As I drew closer to the homes, an idea came to me. Taking out my handkerchief, I held it to my face as if I had a bad tooth ache. It also covered most of my face.

Just as I came to the first house, a man came out of a shed. Seeing me, he said something, which, of course, I didn't understand. Keeping a steady pace, I gave a loud groan, and pointed to my face with my free hand. Laughing, he gave a wave and turned away.

Breathing a sigh of relief, I hurried past the other two houses. Walking in daylight like this was extremely risky, but what else could I do with nowhere to hide?

After another mile or so, a welcome sight came into view—a small hill rising from the left side of the road. Even better were the many clumps of brambles scattered over the hillside. A good hiding place at last! As soon as I reached the hill I climbed through the brambles and found a secluded spot. I lay down and fell into a sleep of sheer exhaustion.

It was late afternoon when I awoke. Cautiously I climbed to the crest of the hill and looked south. In the valley below I saw a small hamlet with a railway station. Hunger, thirst, and weakness were telling me it was time to surrender. Vichy, France, was still at least fifty miles away. Without food and water, I couldn't possibly cover that distance. The hamlet below looked like a good place to "call it a day" and surrender.

But then I saw something that pushed such thoughts from my mind. Leaning against the side of one of the station buildings was a bicycle! With luck, on a bicycle, I could cover the fifty miles before daylight the next day. My heart began to beat faster.

Then I recalled that under the Geneva Convention escaping prisoners of war could be treated as common criminals if caught with stolen property. It was bad enough being a POW in the hands of the *Luftwaffe*. It would be a hundred times worse being in the hands of the Gestapo with no International Red Cross protection. After a moment's debate with myself, I decided to steal the bicycle anyway—if it were still there after dark.

Impatiently I waited for nightfall. As soon as it was quite dark, I made my way down the hill toward the hamlet. Keeping to the shadows cast by the moon, I slowly approached the railway station.

The bicycle was still there!

Silently I lifted the heavy, old bicycle off the ground and carried it away. Wheeling it might have made a noise. As soon as I reached the road, I pedaled away from the hamlet as fast as I could.

Being weak, from time to time I had to stop for a rest. But I was starting to feel confident that, with luck, I would reach the frontier with Vichy, France, before dawn.

Then my luck ran out!

Coming to a steep grade, I found my legs too weak to turn the pedals, so I dismounted and pushed the bike up the short hill. At the top of the hill, I would see that I was about to enter a village. Not wanting to be caught pedaling through the village on a stolen bicycle, I looked for a way around. I spied a narrow dirt track to the left and turned the bicycle into it. The track took a sharp right turn after about a hundred yards and immediately plunged down a very steep incline which I didn't see in the darkness. Caught completely unawares, I careened down the hill out of control. This wild ride ended abruptly when the bike hit a low dirt embankment at the bottom of the hill. I sailed over the handlebars and crashed into some vegetation, which fortunately broke my landing.

Getting up, I gingerly examined myself for injuries. Other than being winded, I was unhurt. Looking around, I found I had landed in a vineyard. I saw the front wheel of the bicycle was hopelessly bent. I was back to walking once again. But first I had to hide the bicycle so that it wouldn't be found for some time. It must not be connected to me when I was recaptured, which now seemed sadly inevitable. I carried the wrecked bicycle deep into the vineyard where it would not be found until the growing season began.

# A BICYCLE AND A VINEYARD

The dirt track led me back to the road on the far side of the village. I continued walking, but my pace was very slow. In desperation I looked at the few houses on the village outskirts. Breaking into a house was as culpable as stealing the bicycle. Logic told me not to do it. But the urge to escape was still powerful, and I knew that if only I could get some food I would be able to make it to the frontier, which might be only thirty miles away.

I crept around a couple of houses, checking windows and doors, ready to run should a dog start barking. At the last house I saw a short flight of stairs leading down to a basement. The handle turned, and the door swung open. With my heart pounding, I slipped inside and quietly shut the door behind me.

The basement had no windows, and it was pitch black inside. I groped around the wall near the door and found a light switch that turned on a single bulb. Hungrily, I looked around, but all the shelves were bare except for one lonely gallon-size can. I grabbed it and hurried to the door. Turning off the light, I cautiously stepped outside and closed the door behind me. Hugging my find to my chest, I hurried down the road with new-found vigor.

Without a can-opener, I figured I would have to pound the can open with a stone (I had forgotten the hacksaw blade in my pocket.) But opening the can by pounding would make noise, so I walked for at least half an hour before stopping to look for a suitable stone. Finding one, I sat beside the road and began hammering the top of the can. After a lot of pounding I was able to make a hole big enough to get at the contents. To my disappointment the can contained pickled gherkins. But gherkins were better than nothing, even though they had little food value. Ravenously I ate a number.

With something in my stomach, I felt better as I continued walking. But my progress was still slow, and I stopped frequently to rest. After several hours the sky began to lighten with the dawn of the third day of my escape. As it got lighter, I saw that once again I was in the middle of flat, barren farmland with nowhere to hide. This time my reaction was not dismay but resignation. Coming to a lone tree by the roadside I stopped for a rest.

# SHOT DOWN!

A sound made me look back in the direction I had come. A young woman was cycling toward me. As she drew near, our eyes met briefly before she quickly looked ahead, leaned forward over the handlebars, and started pedaling faster. Since all young Germans were in the military, she knew I had to be either a deserter or an escaping prisoner. And I knew my attempt to escape was about to end.

Miles ahead I could see a wooded area. But even if I could reach it, it would be too late. The Germans, knowing I was in the area, would mount a large-scale manhunt, and it would be only a matter of time before they found me.

Without thinking of it being incriminating, I picked up the can of gherkins and continued walking wearily along the road. Now that all hope of escape was gone, I had a feeling of relief that my ordeal would soon end. At least I was not surrendering. Circumstances that I could not change were leading to my capture.

After about half an hour I heard the sound of a motorcycle. Resignedly I watched the policeman approach, slow down, and stop.

"*Wer sind sie?*" ("Who are you?") he barked.

Still holding the can of gherkins, I raised my hands shoulder high and replied in my limited school German, "*Ich bin ein Englisher Kriegs-gefangener.*" ("I am an English prisoner of war.")

"*Ihren ausweis.*" ("Your identification.")

Pulling out my kriegie identification tag which I wore around my neck, I showed it to the policeman. With his hand resting on his gun holster he beckoned me to come closer so he could scrutinize it. Satisfied, he motioned me to continue walking while he idled along behind me.

Only now did I think about of the incriminating can of gherkins and wondered how I could get rid it. How foolish of me not to have left the can by the tree! After about half an hour I indicated I needed to rest. By the way I was walking the policeman knew I was in a bad shape. Sympathetically he pointed to the side of the road. I sat down so that I was between the policeman and the can. After a few minutes, when he signaled me to start walking again, I stood up, leaving the can in the ditch. To my relief he did not notice I was no longer carrying the can.

# A BICYCLE AND A VINEYARD

Arriving at a large village about an hour later, I was taken to the jail and interrogated. I told them I belonged to the Royal Air Force and had escaped from Dulag Luft three nights earlier and that my kriegie identification number was 1006.

When I was taken to a cell, I put my hands on my stomach and said, "*Ich bin sehr hungrig. Essen, bitte?*" ("I am very hungry. Food, please?")

The policeman smiled and nodded as he locked the door.

The next ten or twelve minutes seemed like an eternity. But at last the key turned in the lock, and the policeman entered with a tray. As soon as he left, I wolfed down the two slices of rye bread and the piece of sausage. The mug of ersatz coffee was so hot I had to sip it slowly. It was my first drink in two and a half days. Though I could have eaten a lot more, I was surprised how quickly I felt invigorated.

The only piece of furniture in the cell was a narrow wooden bunk with a thin *palliasse* and an army blanket. Daylight came through a small window with two iron bars. The window overlooked a narrow alley. Only when I saw the two bars did I remember the hacksaw blade in my pocket!

Without any further delay I pulled out the blade and started working on one of the bars.

The policeman had told me I would be handed over to the military. If the military did not come until the next day, I knew from the progress I was making on the first bar that I would be out of that cell by midnight.

I was nearly halfway through the first bar when the key rattled in the lock. Quickly I pushed the hacksaw blade under the *palliasse* as I sat on the bunk. The policeman entered with another welcome tray of food. On it were the usual two slices of rye bread, sausage, a pat of creamy margarine, and mug of ersatz coffee.

As soon as I had eaten, I began cutting the bar again. When I was nearly two-thirds of the way through the bar, the key again rattled in the lock. I quickly sat on the bunk, pushing the blade under the *palliasse*. My heart sank as the door opened. Standing behind the policeman were two soldiers with rifles slung across their backs.

"*Raus. Schnell machen*" ("Get up. Be quick."), one of the soldiers barked.

# SHOT DOWN!

Jumping up, I hurried to the door. As I walked out of the cell, one of the soldiers gave me a hard shove from behind. I knew I would have to be very careful with these two young arrogant men! This was the first time I had met Germans like them. I sensed it wouldn't take much to provoke them to some form of brutality.

Escorting me out of the police station, they marched me at a brisk pace through the village to a small railway station. A few villagers looked at me with curiosity. Being still weak, I had difficulty walking as fast as my captors wanted, and an occasional *"Schnell machen"* was accompanied with a rough shove from behind.

A short while later a passenger train pulled into the station. One of the soldiers climbed into a carriage and commandeered a compartment, ordering the civilian occupants out. They then hustled me into the compartment, where I sat on one side while the soldiers sat facing me.

We traveled in silence until the train arrived at Nuestadt. From the railway station I was taken by army truck to a POW camp on the outskirts of the city. During the interrogation I learned this camp was for French POWs. The following day I was handed over to two *Luftwaffe* soldiers, who took me back to Dulag Luft. Arriving there in the afternoon, I was placed in a cell similar to the one in which I had spent those unpleasant thirteen days before my escape.

As I sat on the edge of my bunk, I wondered what kind of punishment I might receive for escaping. But at the same time I felt a deep satisfaction because I had shown the Germans that, for me, the war was not over. And I had tied up some of their resources looking for me.

An hour or so later my cell door opened and the guard announced, "Herr Kommandant."

Jumping to my feet, I snapped to attention and clicked my heels in salute as a smartly dressed officer entered the cell. As he returned my salute, I noticed he wore an Iron Cross on his tunic.

He looked at me for a moment and then totally surprised me by extending his hand. As we shook hands, he said in perfect Oxford English, "Congratulations, Curnow. That was a jolly good show." He smiled at me as I looked at him with my mouth wide open.

"Sit down, Curnow," he said as he sat on the edge of the bunk. He continued, "You are the first prisoner who has ever escaped from my camp over the fence." And with a determined look, he added, "And you will be the last!"

I grinned as I pondered why he would make such a boast.

Pulling out a packet of cigarettes, he said, "Have a fag."

"No thank you, Sir. I don't smoke."

"Oh, come on, Curnow. They're good English Players," he urged, showing me the packet. I wondered how a German was smoking English cigarettes. Later I came to understand that they would have been pilfered from a parcel sent to a POW.

The Players brand was the one I used to smoke, and, in a moment of weakness, I took one. So ended six months of nonsmoking, and eight years of ever increasingly heavy smoking began.

As we sat smoking together, he asked me a few personal questions and then stood up to go. Jumping to attention, I again clicked my heels. Returning my salute, he left my cell, and the door was locked behind him.

I sat back on my bunk amazed. I could hardly believe the way the interview had gone. To be personally congratulated by the camp commandant for escaping was an experience I would never forget.

The next morning I was returned to the camp compound. Then I saw the reason for the commandant's boast that I would be the last prisoner to escape over the fence. He had changed the guard box weaponry from rifles to machine guns. If, five days earlier, the guards had been armed with machine guns, I would not have escaped. With the lights on, I would never have tried to run away from a machine gun. I would have surrendered when Jack Mason was caught. When I looked for Mason I learned that he, with a number of other prisoners, had been transferred to Stalag Luft III, a permanent POW camp.

Over the next few days more survivors from other bombers trickled in until there were about twenty-five of us. Five days after I arrived back at Dulag Luft, we were transported to the railway station at Frankfurt. From there, we traveled under tight security to Stalag Luft III.

# BRIBERY AND BLACKMAIL

Stalag Luft III was situated about one hundred miles southeast of Berlin near the small town of Sagan in Poland. At that time this permanent POW camp consisted of three compounds set in a clearing at the edge of a pine forest. The two larger compounds were for POWs, one occupied by commissioned officers and the other by senior non-commissioned officers (NCOs). Most of the kriegies belonged to the British Royal Air Force, but there were also a number from the Royal Australian, Canadian, and New Zealand Air Forces. The two kriegie compounds were separated by the third compound, the *forlager*, which contained the German administration offices, the guards' barracks, and other ancillary buildings.

When we arrived at Stalag III, we were taken to the administration office, identified, registered, and assigned to various barracks. After being issued with eating utensils and two army blankets, we were marched into the NCO compound and taken to our respective barracks. (I had not yet learned I was a commissioned officer.)

Just inside the entrance of each barrack was a small area partitioned off for cooking purposes. An opening in the middle of the partition led into the main living area. When I entered my barrack, I stood in the cooking area, uncertain what to do next. Just then a kriegie came through the opening in the partition. He looked at me wide-eyed and open-mouthed. Calling back into the living area, he yelled, "Hey, fellows. Come out here."

When several other kriegies appeared, he pointed at me and said,

# BRIBERY AND BLACKMAIL

"What has the RAF come to that they're robbing the cradle?"

The other men laughed, and two or three chorused, "Welcome to kriegieland."

One asked, "How old are you?"

Somewhat defensively, I replied, "Nineteen."

Shaking his head he said, "You look more like sixteen."

All my life I have looked younger than my age. When I was young, I didn't like it, but now that I'm older, I do. After this initial lighthearted banter, the kriegies gathered around, plying me with questions—name, squadron, crew position, how many ops, and many other questions. There were expressions of approval when they learned I had been on a bomber squadron for over six months. (Statistics at the end of the war showed that the average operational life of a Bomber Command crew was only six weeks, or twenty-two operational hours.)

Since food was still uppermost in my mind, I asked about meals. I learned about the weekly food parcels that were supplied through the International Red Cross. These came either from England, Canada, or America. Supplies of bulk food also came periodically from Australia and Argentina. Each food parcel supplied about two thousand calories a day, which, added to the meager German rations, gave the POWs a healthy diet.

At Sagan, before the parcels were distributed, the cans of meat were removed and sent to the kriegie-operated cookhouse. The meat was used in the midday cooked meals, along with German rations of potatoes and occasionally other vegetables.

Our captors also supplied a daily ration of about one inch of very old rye bread (the loaves were embossed with their date which showed them to be ten months or more old). From time to time they gave us some sauerkraut and a small quantity of horse meat. Occasionally, we would be given small, round, flat cheeses, which we called "fish cheese" since their offensive smell reminded us of rotten fish! On principle we accepted it, but instead of eating it, we surreptitiously buried it in the ground.

After I was shown my bunk, I went for a stroll. I was anxious to see the layout of the camp, and also to find Jack Mason. At the camp office I learned that Mason was serving a two-week sentence of solitary confinement for his attempted escape at Dulag Luft. As I continued my stroll around the camp, I wondered when I would be hauled off to the cooler.[1] I never was. Apparently, the commandant never sent through a report of my escape.

The three compounds were surrounded by the usual double barbed wire fencing. Unlike Dulag Luft, there was no roll of barbed wire on the compound side of the fence. However, a single strand of wire, twelve inches above the ground and fifteen feet from the fence, ran the entire circumference of the camp, except at the main gate. This was called the "warning wire." Notices, placed at intervals, reminded us that we could be shot if we stepped over the wire. Even touching it could bring gunfire. A guard had to be called to retrieve any object, such as a ball or cap, which might roll or be blown into this no-man's land. The German *forlager* did not have a warning wire.

*"Goon box by moonlight." A sketch by a POW artist friend at Fallingbostel, 1944.*

Goon boxes[2] were spaced every one hundred yards along the fences. The guards within were armed with machine guns and searchlights which periodically swept the compound during the night. Besides the goons manning the boxes, others patrolled outside the compound with dogs. A few wandered around the camp and through the barracks, on the lookout for suspicious activity. In addition to the goons in regular uniform, special security men, referred to as "ferrets," furtively and quickly slipped around the camp. They were dressed in dark blue overalls, and whenever one was seen entering the compound, the whole camp was alerted. Ferrets were particularly disliked by the krie-gies.

Our compound contained sixteen large wooden barracks, laid out in four rows of four. There was also a large building used as a theater. The camp had an active theatrical society, which periodically performed plays with, of course, all-male casts. It was surprising how makeup would make some of the men look like women. The first show I attended, I thought an attractive young woman was playing the lead female part. When I asked where she came from, other kriegies doubled-up with laughter. To put it mildly, I was embarrassed. That kriegie actor had a more boyish face than I!

One small building housed the camp's sporting equipment and the office of the British camp leader, Dixie Dean, and secretary, Ron Mogg. Lastly, there were two large washroom/toilet buildings, one on either side of the compound. They backed against the warning wire.

The barracks were wooden buildings, eighty feet long by thirty feet wide, and divided into two sections. A doorway connected the two sections, which allowed snooping goons to move quickly through the building. Each section had forty two-tier bunks, arranged in units of four, which made living conditions extremely crowded, and afforded little privacy.

Upper bunks were more popular as they provided plenty of air space. The air space of the lower bunks was only two feet by six feet and three-and-a-half feet high—not a place for anyone suffering from claustrophobia! I was given a lower bunk. The space beneath the lower bunk was shared by both the bottom and top men for storing food parcels, clothing, and other personal items. Each kriegie jealously guarded his space, personalizing it with the few treasured items he possessed. This was now his "home" for the duration of the war. In early 1943 no one knew how long the war would last. Some men had already been kriegies for three years.

The first day I was at Sagan I heard shrill blasts of a whistle around 4:00 P.M. "What's that for?" I asked as everyone started moving out of the barrack. *"Appel,"* I was told.

*Appel* was a parade that was held each morning and afternoon for the purpose of counting the POWs. We stood five deep for easy counting by the Germans. However, the reliability of the count depended upon the cooperation of the POWs, but more about that in the next chapter.

Later that evening I learned that the camp's clandestine radio was in my barrack. Its concealment was a classic example of kriegie ingenuity. Fastened to the wall of the kitchen in every barrack was a first-aid box. In our barrack, hidden hinges allowed the box to swing out, exposing the radio fastened to its back. A hole had been cut in the wall, into which the radio recessed. A concealed peg held the box firmly closed.

The radio's aerial consisted of a sturdy wire strung around the entire barrack room, which also acted as a washing line for the kriegies. When the radio was in use, one end of a connecting wire was threaded through a small hole in the partition and clipped to the main aerial, while the other end was plugged into the radio.

A team of four kriegies operated the radio. One man, wearing earphones, wrote down the BBC news in shorthand; another man stood behind him, ready to snatch off the earphones and push them into the hole should the presence of a goon or a ferret be announced by one of the several watchmen. A third man would disconnect the aerial which would be pulled back through the partition. The fourth man stood ready to slam the box closed and lock it in place. This emergency shut-down took only three seconds.

The usual time for getting the news was 6:00 P.M. Several copies were written out from the shorthand report and a team of readers spread out over the camp. During the course of the evening every barrack was visited. Except for someone keeping watch, everyone would gather around the reader, eager to hear the latest news of the war. With the war turning in favor of the Allies, getting the news from London played an important part in maintaining our morale at a high level. I asked the men how they had obtained the parts for the radio, and they told me a story of intrigue, bribery, and blackmail.

It started by offering a friendly goon a cup of coffee as he wandered through the barrack. The only hot drink he had ever tasted was ersatz coffee. When he was assured that kriegies were on the lookout for any other goon or ferret, the aroma of real coffee proved irresistible, and he sat down to drink some for the first time. The next time he was introduced to cigarettes made from Virginia tobacco. German tobacco was awful. Soon his visits became regular.

The next step was to persuade him to take some chocolate home for his children who had never tasted it before. Meanwhile, every bit of this illegal fraternization with prisoners was being documented. He was now asked to bring in a harmless item like an onion. (I never tasted an onion in the twenty-five months I was a POW, and to this day, I cannot eat too many of them!)

Fritz (a pseudonym) was now trapped and subjected to blackmail. He was threatened with exposure if he didn't cooperate and bring in what was demanded. Up to this point exposure would have led to him being sent to the dreaded Eastern Front. But once he started bringing in the parts for a radio, exposure could well have led to a court martial and a firing squad.

Thanks to Fritz and some ruthless kriegies, we were able to know the true progress of the war and laugh at the propaganda the Germans published in a special news sheet for POWs.

---

[1] The kriegie term for the punishment cells.

[2] "Goon" was the kriegie nickname for a German guard, so the small, raised guard boxes (see picture) became "goon boxes."

# TUNNELING IN SAND

About a week after getting to Sagan I was lying on my bunk when a familiar voice said, "Hi, John. So you didn't make it!"

There by my bunk, with a big grin on his face, stood Jack Mason. After a warm handshake, we went for a stroll together, swapping details of our experiences since the lights at Dulag Luft were turned on accompanied by whistles blowing and shouts of *"Achtung!"* It wasn't long until our conversation turned toward the possibility of escape—again! We looked at the goon boxes, the machine guns, searchlights, and the guards patrolling outside the fence, and we had to admit that escape looked pretty hopeless.

"The only way to get out of this dump would be by a tunnel," Jack sighed, "and I bet there isn't a place that hasn't already been thought of." Nothing was said for a while as we continued walking. We were approaching one of the washroom/toilet buildings when I broke the silence. "I guess you're right, Jack. But let's take a look in here anyway. It's the nearest building to the fence."

In the large washroom two long wash tables ran the width of the room along the walls. Faucets, placed every two or three feet, supplied cold water. Each wash table sloped so that the waste water ran into shallow troughs against the walls. A pipe in the center of each trough allowed the water to drain into sumps in the floor. From the sides of these two sumps, pipes drained the water into a third sump beneath two shorter wash tables in the middle of the room. From this center sump all the water drained into an area between the building and the fence.

# TUNNELING IN SAND

Pointing to one of the sumps I said, "That would be a good place to start a tunnel, except that it's too small for anyone to squeeze through."

Shrugging our shoulders in frustration, we continued our walk around the compound. We hadn't gone far when Mason stopped and said, "John, you may be onto something. Let's go back to the washroom. I want to measure those sumps."

In the washroom, Mason got down on his knees, and using his belt, measured the base of the sump, across and diagonally. Standing up, he told me to put my arms above my head. He then held the belt across my shoulders.

Excitedly, he said, "Any average-sized man could get through that sump if he held his arms above his head. You've hit on a terrific idea." We stood looking at each other with big grins on our faces. A tunnel from the washroom would lead to the *forlager*. We felt that wouldn't be a major problem since the fence around the *forlager* was unlit and unguarded.

The next step was to take our idea to the escape committee. Tunneling was never a one- or two-man job. It required a great deal of planning and a large team of workers. The escape committee thought our idea was a good one, and since no other escape project was under way at the time, it was decided to start work on the tunnel immediately.

The first job was to get a small quantity of cement smuggled into the camp. A little blackmailing in Fritz's direction did the trick. With the cement, a false bottom was made for the sump. When it was ready, the bottom of the cement-lined sump was broken up. The false bottom fit perfectly. Only then could the digging start.

The camp was built on a deep, firm layer of fine sand, which meant the digging would be fairly easy. But what would we do with the excavated sand? Each barrack room had two large metal water jugs, and someone was always carrying two jugs of water from the washroom to a barrack. Once the digging started, some of those jugs were filled with sand, instead of water. The guards didn't notice the moderate increase of this traffic, and their suspicions were not aroused.

In the spaces between the barracks, kriegies scraped away the dirty top layer of sand, exposing clean sand like that coming from the tunnel. Shallow sandpits were made, ostensibly for sunbathing.

Now that it was May and the sun was warming up, this also did not arouse any suspicion. When no goons or ferrets were in the camp, the jugs of sand were passed out through windows and the sand spread around in the sunbathing pits. Collecting and dispersing the sand required the cooperation of the whole camp.

A complicated warning system was set up so that everyone involved with the tunnel work knew within seconds when a goon or ferret entered the camp. This system involved the opening and closing of windows in key positions. Mason and I were assigned to the team operating the warning system. The digging was left to more experienced men.

At first the work was slow. The diggers had to lie on the washroom floor and reach down to scoop out the sand, one cupful at a time. The deeper the hole became, the harder it was to do this. However, once the hole was big enough for someone to get into it, the digging speeded up. The diggers were then able to hand up sand by the jugful.

The first stage was to dig a shaft down about twelve feet. The tunnel had to be at least twelve feet deep so that the seismographs placed along the fence at regular intervals wouldn't detect the digging. When they reached this depth the diggers widened the shaft into a large chamber, measuring about ten feet by ten feet and some eight feet high. A big escape was planned, so the chamber had to be large enough to hold all the kriegies who would be involved. It took two or three weeks to excavate this chamber.

As the work progressed, the diggers were constantly faced with the problem of the sandy soil caving in. To prevent this, they used boards to shore up the sides and roof of the tunnel. Each kriegie was asked to contribute one of his bed boards.[1]

Another problem was having an adequate supply of air at the face of the tunnel. Workers rigged up a pair of bellows, made out of a canvass kitbag, to pump the air through a pipe. The pipe was made of empty powdered-milk cans. More sections of pipe were added as the tunnel grew longer. To meet the constant demand for cans, prisoners brought cans, with the bottoms already cut out, to the washroom in the empty water jugs. Even with this system for pumping air into the tunnel, the diggers could work only short shifts.

The workers used a box with ropes attached front and back to haul the sand from the tunnel face. With one rope the digger pulled the empty box to the tunnel face. When he had filled it, he would give a tug on the other rope. Another member of the digging crew would then pull the full box back to the chamber. Another important rope was the one attached to the ankles of the digger so he could be pulled back quickly from the tunnel face. This would be critical in

*A typical POW tunnel*

the event of a cave-in. These diggers were courageous men!

To provide lighting in an otherwise pitch-black environment, Fritz was bribed and blackmailed into supplying the necessary electric wire and socket. The bulb was borrowed from a barrack. The wire was connected to the washroom wiring only when work was in progress. If a goon showed up unexpectedly, the warning system alerted the workers and they would quickly disconnect the wire and pass it down into the chamber. Sometimes the digging team did not have enough time to get out, and they would have to remain in the chamber in total darkness until the all clear was given.

Meanwhile, life in the camp went on as normal. That is, until a boneheaded kriegie snatched the cap off the head of a goon. He got away only because other kriegies quickly crowded around the goon. The German authorities demanded that the cap be returned immediately and the culprit be turned over for punishment. Naturally, Dixie Dean, the British camp leader, refused this demand. The Germans responded by shutting down the camp theater and all sporting activities. Extra *appels* were also called at random times, including meal times. These measures were countered with total lack of cooperation by the kriegies. Which side would give in first? After several days, a big cheer went up when Dixie Dean announced that a compromise had been reached. The Germans caved. They said they would discontinue all their restrictive measures if the cap was returned, without the culprit being surrendered.

During this time work on the tunnel was suspended because goons and ferrets were constantly on the prowl. However, as soon as things returned to normal, the work quickly forged ahead.

About this time we received disturbing news. With the mounting Allied air offensive against Germany, an increasing number of airmen were being shot down and captured. This led the Germans to reorganize their POW camp program. They decided to use our compound for American Air Force officers, and transfer us to a new camp at Heydekrug, near the frontier of East Prussia and the Baltic country of Lithuania.

Our initial plan was to dig the tunnel obliquely from the washroom, in order to bypass the soak area where the soil would be unstable. The completed tunnel would be about 120 feet long and end at a woodshed in the *forlager.* However, because of the impending move to Heydekrug, there wouldn't be time to complete such a long tunnel. It was therefore decided to dig straight out to the fence. That would shorten the tunnel by at least two-thirds. It was a gamble, since it meant going through the soak area. But it was either this or abandon the project altogether.

The Germans planned to move the three thousand POWs from Sagan to the new camp, using a special passenger train. The train would shuttle six times between the two camps, carrying about five hundred men each time. Since it would take three weeks to complete the first five round trips, we believed we would have enough time to complete the tunnel—provided we could make it through the soak area. As the evacuation and transfer progressed, those who were involved in the tunnel project moved to other barracks whenever their own barracks were scheduled to be transferred to the new camp.

The next two weeks were tense ones as the tunnel slowly lengthened. Then our worst fears were realized. There was a cave-in. The soil above the tunnel poured in like quicksand and a hole about three feet in diameter and two feet deep appeared on the surface, halfway between the washhouse and the fence. Fortunately, the digging shift was being changed and there was no one at the face of the tunnel. If a digger had been trapped it would have been a disaster. The men in the chamber quickly climbed out and all signs of the work were cleaned away before the Germans detected the hole and cordoned off the building.

A large group of kriegies stood around, watching as several goons probed the ground with a long metal rod. Some officers and ferrets spent a lot of time thoroughly examining the inside of the building. Finally the Germans decided the ground had subsided due to the waste water, and after filling the hole with a load of dirt, they withdrew.

The next day the digging crew began the task of digging out the tunnel where the cave-in had occurred. This time they used a lot more boards to shore up the tunnel. Two or three days later the shoring had just been completed when the man digging at the face of the tunnel saw sand start to flow into the tunnel. He yelled, "Cave-in" as he tugged urgently on the emergency rope and started to wriggle backwards. Quickly he was pulled back, just in time to avoid being engulfed by the sand that poured, once more, into the tunnel. It was now obvious that our gamble had failed; the tunnel project was over.

Once again a hole appeared on the surface, in the same place. The Germans now realized there had to be a tunnel. They again cordoned off the building and spent a lot of time searching—unsuccessfully— for the tunnel entrance. Finally they decided to dig down from the outside to find the tunnel. A crowd of kriegies, watching from a distance, cheered gleefully when the sides of the pit being dug caved in. The Germans eventually shored up the sides of the pit with planks and continued digging. Finally the goon at the bottom announced he had found the tunnel. The officer in charge told him to crawl back down the tunnel to the entrance. The officer and the others then went into the building to see where the goon would emerge. We learned later that the Germans had gasped in amazement when the bottom of the sump lifted and the goon's head appeared.

And so, for us kriegies, the war was *not* over, although for us the war was now one of wits rather than guns.

---

[1] Each bunk had about eight bed boards to support the straw-filled *palliasse*. Giving up one of the boards increased the gap between the remaining boards.

# A CORNFIELD IN POLAND

About a week later, at the evening *appel,* we were told that the transfer train was back and the rest of us would be leaving the next day. Everywhere, the camp was a hive of activity as we kriegies packed our few possessions. We could take only what we could carry.

For me packing was a simple task since, in the three months I had been a POW, I had accumulated very few possessions. It was now the end of June 1943, and I celebrated my twentieth birthday in a POW camp. The past year—my last as a teenager—had been incredible. So much had happened in my life since I arrived at Lichfield and Tatenhill.

For some time I had been preparing for my next escape, either by the tunnel or from the train should the tunnel project fail. I had retailored my battledress jacket to make it look more civilian and had fashioned a satchel using material from an old discarded uniform. I now filled the satchel with my few toilet items, a small towel, shoe polish and rag, and, most importantly, a supply of dried food.

From my weekly food parcels I had been saving some rolled oats, sugar, cocoa, and condensed milk. After the tunnel caved in the second time, I mixed all these ingredients into a thick paste that I dried into a half-inch-thick "cake," which I then cut into bars. If I should be able to escape, I was determined not to be caught again without food. I felt I was well prepared for another crack at freedom.

There was one other important item in my satchel—a small iron bar. I don't remember now how I obtained this. It was sharpened and narrowed at one end to act as a screwdriver. It could also be used as a small crowbar.

The next morning we lined up in a long column, flanked by numerous guards, and marched to the Sagan railway station. Before we boarded the waiting train, the German commandant addressed us briefly in excellent English. He boasted about the security and how there had been no trouble from the POWs on the previous five trips. He warned us to behave and give no trouble to the guards. His self-confidence only increased my determination to get off that train if at all possible. Because Jack Mason had been housed in a different barrack, we were not together.

Boarding the train, I made my way to the center of the car I was in, so as to be as far away as possible from the guards stationed at either end by the doors. The seats had high backs with luggage racks above them, so the guards could see what was going on in the center of the car only if they came down the aisle.

Finding the window seats already taken, I asked the kriegies occupying them whether they were planning to escape. They said they weren't, so when I told them I was, and therefore needed a window seat, one of them relinquished his seat.

Our carriage was an old, wooden one; its windows were raised and lowered by a leather strap. To stop the windows from being opened, the Germans had used four security measures. First, they had driven a large bolt into the coachwork below the window to keep it from being lowered. Next, they had placed six screws through the sash and window frames, three on either side. Third, they had jammed wooden wedges between the sash and window frames on each side of the window. And finally, they had twisted thick wire around two bolts, one of which had been driven into the coachwork above the window, and the other into the top of the window.

I thought how unnecessary all that was. All they really needed to do was to place one bolt under each window—*driven in from the outside of the car where the kriegies couldn't get at it.* As it was, all their security measures were accessible to active kriegie fingers.

After about an hour, the train slowly pulled out of Sagan station. The twenty-four-hour journey would take us northeast across Poland

and into what was then East Prussia. Our final destination was Stalag Luft 6 near the small town of Heydekrug, only a few miles from the Baltic Sea.

Once the train was underway, I gave closer attention to the window. I was surprised to find that the bolt under my window was missing, as were three of the six screws fastening the window to the sash. I was further excited to find that the wedges were only finger-tight and that the twisted coil of wire was hanging loosely on the two bolts. Obviously, some kriegie had been hard at work during one of the previous trips. And just as obviously the Germans had failed to carry out any security inspections, either due to slackness or overconfidence. I could hardly believe my good fortune. All I had to do was remove the remaining three screws and the window would be ready to open.

I was thankful I had my iron bar. Since it was not a proper screwdriver I had to be very careful not to tear up the slots in the screws. Just one unextracted screw would hold the window fast. It was a slow, painstaking, arduous task. But as I worked on the last screw, the kriegies sitting near me caught some of my excitement. Eventually, I gave that screw a couple of final turns with my fingers and held it up in triumph; they gave a subdued cheer.

"OK, Curnow," one of them said. "So you can open the window now. But how do you plan to get away, with the train charging along at fifty miles an hour? It has slowed down only twice all day when it stopped to take on coal and water, and then the goons were everywhere outside."

"I'm hoping it will slow down just once during the night so I can jump out. If not . . ." I shrugged my shoulders.

During the rest of the afternoon, I dozed off and on. When night fell, I pulled out the four wedges and removed the wire from the two bolts. All that was left was to lower the window.

While the rest of the men slept, I fought to keep awake. I didn't want to miss any chance of escaping if the train slowed down. But except for one well-guarded stop during the night for refueling, the train continued to travel at a fast speed. Disappointedly I watched the eastern sky begin to lighten with the dawn.

One by one the other kriegies awoke from their night's sleep, and I wasn't very happy when one of them teased me about still being there. About half an hour later, we began to slow down as the engine labored heavily to pull the train up a fairly steep grade. Our speed became slower and slower, and my frustration grew greater and greater. "Why couldn't this have happened two hours ago when it was still dark?" I moaned.

Then a wonderful sight came into view. Growing down the hillside, right to the edge of the railway track, was a field of tall corn—at least six feet tall. My heart started to beat faster as I looked at this dense growth no more than ten feet from the train. With no fence to climb, I could be out of sight in seconds. I knew this would be my only chance to escape.

I quietly lowered the window by its strap. Then, crouching for a moment in the opening, I dropped my satchel. Then I jumped after it and rolled as I hit the ground. One of the guards saw me and sounded the alarm. Although the satchel containing my precious food supply was close, I realized it would be fatal to try to retrieve it. Jumping up, I plunged quickly into the cornfield before the guard could grab his rifle and take aim.

I could hear the train grinding to a stop and knew that a guard must have pulled the chain that activated the emergency brakes. But I also knew that the goons had five hundred other kriegies to guard and that it was unlikely that they would try searching for me in the cornfield. I would be like the proverbial needle in a haystack. But I knew something else. I knew there was a machine gun mounted on a flatbed railway car attached to the train. Any movement in the cornfield would make an easy target for the machine gunner. So I quickly lay down flat on the ground, hardly daring to breathe because I was only about thirty yards from the shouting guards.

After about five minutes, the engineer blew the whistle, and the train slowly chugged up the hill. I continued lying on the ground until the sound of the train died away. Even in this situation, I relished the exquisite exhilaration that only an escaping kriegie could experience. Once again I was tasting freedom—freedom to walk a mile, or two, or more, without being hemmed in with barbed wire.

But my euphoria was short-lived; I remembered my lost satchel and realized I had made a foolish mistake by not stashing my food supply in my pockets. Again, I was trying to escape without food. I consoled myself that I was in Poland where, if I was careful, I might get help. Besides, this was no time to worry about food. I had to get away from the area quickly. Already the local authorities might have been notified by radio of my escape and be organizing a search party. I walked through the cornfield to the top of the escarpment that had slowed the train. Ahead the land was flat and under heavy cultivation. Unlike my escape in late March, when the farmland was barren, I now had ample hiding places.

Skirting the edges of fields and avoiding the few country lanes I came to, I walked in a northerly direction. But after several hours, having been awake the previous night, I was too tired to continue. Finding a secluded spot, I lay down and was soon asleep.

I awoke in the late afternoon feeling refreshed. Before going any farther, I had to determine, if possible, approximately where I was. I knew I was in Poland, but where? My goal was the port city of Danzig (Gdansk) on the Baltic Sea. But should I head northwest, north, or northeast? Thankful that I still had my escape maps in the waistband of my trousers, I pulled out the one of Central Europe. As I studied it, I was able to trace the railway line from Sagan and follow its route across Poland. When I jumped from the train, I had been traveling about half the time it was supposed to take to get to the new camp. So I believed I must be somewhere near the city of Thorn (Torun). And since the train hadn't yet reached that important railway junction, I had to be somewhere to the southwest of the city. Thus Danzig must be about a hundred miles due north.

In England, we had been told that some of the captains of the neutral Swedish ships stopping at Danzig would help an escapee, provided he could get aboard the ship and hide without being seen. Only after the ship had put to sea should the escapee make his presence known. These friendly ships could be identified by the special order in which certain clothing was hanging on a washing line. We had committed this "secret code" to memory.

I placed the map back in its hiding place and continued walking along the pathways between fields of various grains, much of it tall corn. I was happy when I eventually came to a road, as it would have been difficult walking through cultivated farmland at night. I hadn't gone far along the road, when, in the fading twilight, I saw a small hamlet about a quarter of a mile ahead. Crouching low, I cut across a field of rye to a nearby thicket of trees. I could see that the nearest cottage was set back from the road and situated a short distance from the rest of the cottages. Could I get some food there?

I sat leaning against a tree until it was completely dark; it was a moonless night. Slowly and cautiously, I moved toward the cottage. The night was so dark that I could make out the outline of the house only when I was very close. I strained my ears for the slightest sound. Satisfied there was no one around, I stealthily approached the cottage and tapped softly on the door. After a tense moment, the door opened a few inches. In the dim light behind her, I could see the apprehensive face of a woman.

Hoping she could understand German, I quietly said, *"Ich bin ein Englisch Flieger"* ("I am an English flyer"), I said quietly. *"Ich bin ein Kriegsgefangener."* ("I am a prisoner of war.")

She quickly closed the door. Disappointed, I was about to turn away, when the door again opened, this time wider. The room was in darkness. As the woman cautiously peered around in the darkness, I reassured her in my limited German that no one had seen me.

Whispering in German, *"Kommen sie rein"* ("Come inside"), she took hold of my arm and pulled me in. Closing and locking the door, she turned the light back on.

In the small, dimly lit, and sparsely furnished room, I saw a young girl, twelve or thirteen years old, standing by a table with a few chairs. Turning to the brave Polish woman, I saw she was gazing at me intently, with both fear and compassion in her eyes. In her mid-thirties, she was dressed in the plain, coarse clothing of a hard-working peasant.

I smiled and, with my hand on my tummy, said, *"Ich bin sehr hungrig."* ("I am very hungry.")

Relaxing, she returned my smile and motioned me to one of the chairs by the table. She then disappeared into the tiny kitchen while her daughter stood shyly looking at me. The mother returned with a thick slice of rye bread, a pat of margarine, and a mug of ersatz coffee.

As I ate, she stood quietly, but nervously, watching. I sensed that she was anxious for me to leave.

Standing up, I warmly thanked her for the food, which she had obviously given from very meager resources. With a slow nod, she gave a sad smile and then hurried to the door and turned off the light. Opening the door, she stepped outside to make sure no one was around. Satisfied that all was clear, she whispered for me to come. Taking her hand in both of mine, I squeezed it gently to express my deepest gratitude before she retreated into the cottage and quickly closed the door. With my back against the wall, I silently slipped to the end of the cottage and melted into the night, confident that I had not compromised this Polish heroine.

As my eyes once more grew accustomed to the blackness, I was surprised how much light came from the stars shining brightly in the cloudless sky. I was able to see the outlines of trees and other objects, which helped me to skirt around the hamlet and back to the road.

With renewed vigor I strode along the road, pondering the amazing courage of this Polish mother. I had seen no evidence of a husband and father. Had he been killed in the Nazi rape of Poland? Or had the Germans conscripted him to fight on the Eastern Front? This brave Polish woman had given me no hint. Her kindness and bravery in the face of certain death had she been caught helping me, has endeared the Polish people to my heart all through the years. I was proud my country had declared war against the Nazis when they invaded her noble and ancient country.

As I walked through the night, I was happy the North Star showed that the road was taking me in a northerly direction. However, at dawn the road turned east, probably leading to Thorn. It grew lighter, and I knew it was time to look for a suitable hiding place to spend the daylight hours.

In about half an hour I came to a dirt road to the left heading north. I turned and took this road. Before long I started to pass a field of tall corn growing about fifty feet from the road. *A good hiding place,* I thought. Just then I saw the road led to a small farmhouse with a barn and one or two sheds. Maybe because of extreme tiredness, both mental and physical, I threw aside all caution and decided to see if the farmer would help me. Such a decision didn't make sense; it was contrary to all the rules for escapees—especially in the daylight.

As I entered the farmyard, I heard a dog growling. Startled, I looked toward the nearby barn. Standing glaring at me was the farmer, who looked as mean as the medium-sized mongrel at his side.

*"Wer sind sie?"* ("Who are you?") *"Was vollen sie?"* ("What do you want?") he demanded harshly in German.

My heart sank. How foolish of me! I should have realized that after the invasion the Germans would have taken over the farms as part of their plunder.

The sight of the dog baring its teeth precluded any thought of running away. Seeing my hesitation, the farmer shouted something in German to his wife in the farmhouse. Quickly she came running with a pistol. As she handed it to her husband, I raised my hands above my head and said, *"Ich bin ein Kriegsgefangener."* Once again I was looking down the barrel of a pistol with an enemy finger on the trigger.

The farmer signaled me to walk to the farmhouse, at the same time speaking rapidly to his wife, who hurried down the dirt road.

Inside the house the farmer motioned me to sit on a chair and place both my hands flat on the kitchen table, while he sat opposite me with his pistol pointing at my heart. Because he was nervous and jittery, it was with considerable uneasiness that I sat watching his finger curled around the trigger. Whenever I looked up, the cold, hard eyes told me he would have no qualms in pulling the trigger if I made a false move.

The next hour—the longest I had ever spent—dragged by in total silence. At last I heard voices and approaching footsteps. With relief I saw a German soldier come through the door, followed by the farmer's wife. The farmer immediately started talking rapidly to the soldier, gesticulating toward me with his pistol. Catching the soldier's eye, I pointed to the pistol. With a nod of his head he told the farmer to put away his pistol. As I gave a heavy sigh of relief, the soldier grinned at me and said scornfully, "Civilian."

After a few more words with the farmer, the soldier turned to me and nodding toward the door, said, *"Geht!"* ("Go!") As I stood up, he tapped the butt of his rifle meaningfully.

As I walked back down the dirt road, with the soldier a few paces behind me, I saw a man in the battledress of a Tommy (British soldier) working near the field of corn. (By the Geneva Convention, any prisoner below the rank of sergeant was required to work.)

"Are you a British kriegie?" I asked.

"Yeah, Dunkirk, 1940. What are you?"

"RAF," I replied.

"Best of luck, mate."

*I'm not having much luck,* I thought as we continued down the road. How different things would have been if that Tommy had been working there an hour or so earlier.

Arriving at the paved road we turned left toward, I believed, the city of Thorn. Though I was tired and hungry, the German soldier kept me marching along at a fast pace. After about half an hour we turned down a side road toward a POW camp.

The soldier took me to the administrative building for interrogation by the camp commandant. After showing him my POW identity tag, and giving him my name, number, and rank, the officer said in very good English, "No. Your name is not Curnow, it is Kernofski and you are a Polish spy. We will have to hand you over to the Gestapo!"

I felt a brief moment of panic, but then saw the twinkle in his eyes. I grinned in response to his teasing and laughingly said, "Kernofski! That's a good one." He smiled as he told me that he had heard about my escape from the train.

I was not put into a solitary confinement cell but taken to a POW barrack room where I met a few more Tommies. They had all been captured at Dunkirk after their heroic stand against overwhelming odds. Holding that thin line of defense had allowed the bulk of the British army to get back to England. I learned from them that the nearby town was indeed Thorn.

The next day, two *Luftwaffe* guards arrived to take me to the new POW camp at Heydekrug. We arrived there later that day and, after a brief interrogation, I was taken to the punishment block to serve a fourteen-day sentence of solitary confinement on bread and water. It was a miserable experience, but at least there was no repeat of the "hot and cold" treatment I had received at the Dulag Luft interrogation center.

# A PHONOGRAPH AND AN ICE RINK

When my two-week stint in the cooler ended, I was taken to the British office inside the camp. There I learned that Jack Mason had reserved a bunk for me in his barrack room. There I received a warm welcome from Mason, who also introduced me to Eric Spong. Eric became a close friend until the end of the war.

The barracks at Heydekrug were quite different from those at Sagan. At Heydekrug, eight long brick buildings, each divided, in turn, into eight rooms, housed fifty-six men in each room, under crowded conditions. Ventilation was very poor, as each room had only two windows and a door at either end. Since most of the men smoked, the atmosphere was terrible. I was happy that Mason and Spong had gotten double bunks next to one of the windows.

After telling Mason about my recent adventures, I asked about the chances of escaping from Heydekrug. "None," he replied. "By the time we arrived a tunnel had already been started and I was told there was no room for any more men. I guess we'll have to wait for the Ruskies (Russians) to liberate us. The tide is beginning to turn on the Eastern Front. Look at this map."

In every room there were numerous crudely drawn maps depicting the Eastern Front. Through the BBC news reports picked up by the clandestine shortwave radio, we were able to keep the maps up-to-date. On the Russian side of the front, the maps were shaded red, and as the Russians advanced westward, more of the map was shaded. The radio reports also told us that the Germans had been

defeated in North Africa and that the Allies, after invading and occupying Sicily, had invaded Italy. These positive reports kept our
morale high as the months slowly dragged by.

Since we openly displayed our maps the Germans knew there
had to be a radio somewhere in the camp. After two or three months
of snooping, the ferrets narrowed its location to the correct room.
Then one afternoon in late autumn, the Germans made a sudden
raid. After stationing guards by the doors at either end of the room,
they ordered all the occupants outside. Two kriegies who understood German remained inside to witness the search. Having POW
observers was required by international law and also protected the
ferrets from accusations of theft or unnecessary damage.

Working their way through the room, the ferrets meticulously
searched every box, container, nook, and cranny. As the search progressed and they failed to find the radio, they became increasingly
frustrated. Then one of them saw a small, portable phonograph on a
shelf. As the guard examined it, one of the kriegie observers heard
him say to another ferret, "I wonder if the radio is inside this."

"Break it open and see," the other suggested.

At this, the observer reminded them that, according to international law, they would be responsible for the damage and would have
to replace the phonograph. He then suggested that they play a record to see if it was a genuine phonograph. Soon the sound of jazz
filled the room. In frustration, the ferret returned it to the shelf.

The kriegie observer breathed an imperceptible sigh of relief.
The radio was inside that phonograph!

Baffled, the Germans withdrew. They had been certain the radio
was in that room. They never found it, and we continued to get the
daily BBC news report from London.

After several months the tunnel project was completed. Its entrance was cleverly hidden behind a stove in the washroom and toilet building located on the far side of the quadrangle, next to the
warning wire. Unfortunately, the diggers miscalculated the length
of the tunnel and broke through to the surface in open ground between the fence and a wooded area. Only a few kriegies escaped
before the Germans discovered what was happening and trapped

the rest of the would-be escapees in the tunnel. There was an immediate lockdown in the barracks.

The next day the "fun and games" began. Naturally, the leaders among the prisoners wouldn't tell the Germans who or how many men had escaped; that was up to them to find out. The Germans called an early *appel,* and we all gathered in the quadrangle, falling in by rooms and standing five deep for easy counting. However, the accuracy of the counting depended upon the cooperation of the kriegies, and on this occasion our captors were not going to get that cooperation! Here and there, after a room had been counted, a diversion was made. While the attention of the goons was distracted, a man would slip quickly to the next group of kriegies and so be counted twice. After two or three counts, each with a different number, the angry officer dismissed the parade.

Later in the morning, with whistles blowing, scores of goons marched into the compound. We were all herded into the quadrangle which was situated at the end of the barracks. Some of the goons then formed a human chain across the compound separating us from the barracks. Meanwhile other goons thoroughly searched the barracks to make sure all the kriegies were in the quadrangle. When they were satisfied the barracks were empty, more goons formed a gauntlet between two lines of barracks. At the other end of the barracks the gauntlet connected with another line of goons that stretched from fence to fence.

Then, we were ordered to march in single file through the gauntlet to be counted. As we passed the several counters, we confused them by repeating several times, in German, numbers they had already counted. Needless to say, each counter came up with a different total.

In the afternoon there was more whistle blowing and, under heavy armed guard, we were all marched into the *forlager* (the German administration compound). After the vacated kriegie compound was again thoroughly searched, we were marched, in single file, back into our compound, being counted as we passed through the gate. Again the counters came up with different totals. The Germans finally gave up!

*Teutonic logic: If you can't find the tunnel entrance, then cave it in! Drawn in my POW wartime log at Heydekrug.*

The whole thing was an hilarious charade, conducted—as far as the kriegies were concerned—in a carnival-like atmosphere.

After two or three days Dixie Dean, our camp leader, informed the camp commandant, Oberst (colonel) Hoermann von Hoerbach, who had escaped. This was advisable so that if and when the escapees were recaptured they would be able to identify themselves as POWs from Heydekrug. Though Colonel Hoerbach was a stern, strict, Prussian officer, he was fair-minded and always treated us as military men, according to the Geneva Convention.

One day, after the tunnel escape, our captors came up with another security measure. They thought it would be a good idea to drive a heavy steamroller around the compound, between the fence and the warning wire, so as to collapse any tunnel we might be building. We roared with laughter as the steamroller got bogged down in the soft ground and had to be dug out. That idea was quickly abandoned.

Summer passed into chilly autumn and, at fifty-five degrees north latitude (the same as Hudson Bay), Old Man Frost and the frigid winds of winter soon embraced the land and brought outdoor sports to a stop—except for the few hardy kriegies who had somehow obtained ice skates. They carefully leveled a part of the quadrangle near the wash/toilet block, making a low mound of dirt around its edges. Then they flooded this area, and by morning the water was frozen. They repeated for several nights until the ice was thick enough to support the skaters. The rest of us were glad to stay inside the barracks, venturing out into the bitter cold only for the morning and evening appels and quick visits to the wash/toilet block.

A major winter pastime was bridge. Jack Mason, Eric Spong, Ernest Lander (a pseudonym), and I played an unending game of bridge for hours each day. The game lasted much of the winter, and the score, if I remember correctly, reached into the thousands.

*"Interminable Bridge." Drawn in my POW wartime log at Heydekrug by a kriegie artist.*

Many of the Red Cross food parcels we received at Heydekrug were English, in which the items were packed in shredded paper. I put my name down for a sack of this paper "wool" and was happy to receive it before the onset of winter. I sewed my two thin blankets together and, folding them into three layers, made a double sleeping bag. I then stuffed the paper into one of the bags. This was better than an electric blanket and kept me warm even on the coldest nights. Several times I awoke in the morning to find snow had blown in through the open window and covered the foot of my homemade sleeping bag. But the insulation was so good that none of the snow melted nor were my feet cold. My bunkmates and I had rearranged our two double bunks, turning them at right angles to the end wall. One bunk was on either side of the window, which, in spite of the cold, we kept open for ventilation.

Finally the long winter gave way to spring; the ice rink melted; and the playing cards were put away. I don't think I have played a game of bridge since. Once again various sporting activities became the norm, and kriegies by the hundreds, in groups or singly, could be seen beating a pathway around the perimeter of the camp. Once again groups of escape-minded kriegies, including Jack Mason and myself, gathered to discuss various possibilities, however crazy some of the ideas might have been.

# SHOT DOWN!

In his article "The Great Escape," Rob Davis, a kriegie at the Sagan camp, wrote, "Security was strict, but life was not intolerable, except for those for whom escape was a restless itch . . . this was reckoned to be just 25 percent of the camp population, and only 5 percent of those were considered to be dedicated escapers." I guess Mason and I were among the 5 percent.

One afternoon in late March 1944, a special *appel* was called. As we gathered around the quadrangle, we wondered what it was all about. A few minutes later Dixie Dean, our camp leader, and the German commandant marched to the center of the square. Calling for silence, Dean said, "The commandant has an announcement to make. Please give him your full attention."

We had never experienced anything like this before. Silently we looked at each other questioningly.

We could see Oberst Hoerbach was tense and looked very grave. Seeking for words, he finally said, "Gentlemen, I have received a very serious report." He went on to tell us that the RAF officers at Stalag Luft III (the camp from which we had transferred the previous year) had, on the night of March 24-25, successfully completed a tunnel, leading to a mass escape of seventy-eight officers.

Pausing to control his emotions, Colonel Hoerbach informed us that fifty recaptured officers had been shot by the Gestapo on orders from Hitler. For a moment there was stunned silence and then loud booing started and continued for several minutes. When we finally quieted down, the commandant, a professional and honorable soldier, well-respected by the kriegies, stressed that the *Luftwaffe* was in no way involved. Naturally, he dared not openly criticize the Nazis. The parade was then dismissed. My squadron lost two fine officers: Squadron Leader I. K. P. Cross, DFC, and Flight Lieutenant G. E. McGill, a Canadian. I must make it clear that the *Luftwaffe* should not be confused with the Nazi SS or Gestapo.

This epic escape, which created a *Grossfahndung* (national alert), is known in prisoner-of-war history as "The Great Escape." Of the seventy-eight officers who exited the tunnel before it was discovered by a patrolling guard, fourteen successfully made it to freedom. Hitler, who had become incensed over the escape, gave orders that all the recaptured escapees be shot and cremated. Of the sixty-four who were recaptured, fourteen were spared, thanks to Goering, Feldmarshall Keitel, and two other generals, who put pressure on the irate Fuhrer. Nine other officers who were waiting in the tunnel made it back to the barracks. The plan was for 220 POWs to escape through this tunnel, which was nicknamed "Harry." I believe it was providential that the tunnel exit was discovered early. Otherwise, the total murdered could have been as many as two hundred.

This terrible news put a complete damper on escaping, as it was now apparent that doing so carried with it the possibility, if not the probability, of being murdered by the Gestapo if recaptured.

Out of boredom I volunteered to work at ironing shirts in the laundry that was situated in the German *forlager*. I was allowed to work there only on condition that I not try to escape. A major advantage of working in the laundry was that every week I was able to get a hot bath. The bath tub was half of a large barrel, and several of us took turns—using the same water. I remember the luxury of my first tub bath in the camp, the first I had had since being shot down.

Soon our minds were fully occupied with the successes the Allies were having in their spring offensives. With the Russians advancing rapidly on the Eastern Front, there was much speculation as to whether they would reach our camp before the Germans had time to evacuate us.

Then in early June came the long-awaited news—the invasion of Europe from the west had begun. D-Day—Deliverance Day—one never to be forgotten! Four long years earlier, the British Expeditionary Force had been driven from continental Europe at Dunkirk. Now that army was back, and, with the mighty American army, would help drive the Germans back to Berlin.

The atmosphere in the camp was euphoric. On our maps of Europe we now started to show the Allied advances from both the west and the east. From time to time goons would quietly come into our barracks and look at our maps to see how the war was going. Nazi propaganda kept them, and all of Germany, in the dark.

# RETREAT FROM THE EASTERN FRONT

In mid-July all speculation about whether we would be liberated by the Russians came to an end. The Germans informed us we were going to be evacuated. We were given three days notice and told we could take only what we could carry on the ten-mile march to the railway station.

One or two kriegies made crude wheelbarrows with wooden wheels. Those didn't last long on the bumpy road. Others teamed up in pairs and carried their belongings either on stretchers or slung over poles that they carried on their shoulders. The rest of us carried either backpacks or kitbags, besides other sundry small packages. Most kriegies overestimated their carrying capability, and after a few miles the roadside became littered with abandoned packages. The kriegie artist's impression on page 155 portrays the different ways in which we endeavored to carry all our worldly possessions. Sadly, I emptied the paper "wool" from my "sleeping bag" and stuffed the two blankets into the crude backpack I had made for the journey. I made sure I had room for my meager food store.

We arrived at the railway station, tired, hungry, and footsore, where we learned the gloomy news that we would be traveling in closed freight cars—not in passenger cars as we had when we transferred from Sagan to Heydekrug. The guards herded us like cattle into the railway cars, forty kriegies in each car. I think horses would have been treated better than we were.

Each car was divided by barbed wire into three sections. The guards occupied the center section with the two doors, one on each side of the car. Twenty kriegies were crowded into each of the other two sections. There was not enough room to lie down; we could sit only with difficulty, and to do that we had to sit on our packs and belongings. We spent a lot of the time standing up.

There were no provisions for drinking water, toilets, or washing. So, in the hot summer weather, we knew we were in for an extremely miserable experience. We didn't know where we were being taken, so we had no idea how long

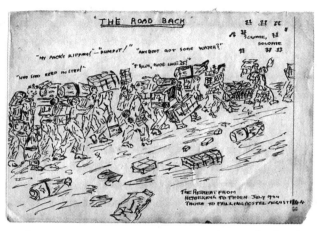

*"The Retreat Begins." Drawn in my wartime log at Fallingbostel.*

we would be imprisoned in these hellish conditions. With elbows sticking into one's back or ribs, it wasn't long before signs of shortening tempers began to appear.

The first leg of the grim train journey lasted about thirty hours and took us to Thorn, some 270 miles to the southwest in Poland. From the Thorn railway station we were marched to the same nearby Stalag to which I had been taken after my escape the previous year.

Our three-week stopover at Thorn was interesting. Jack Mason and I pooled our small personal supplies of cigarettes and purchased a loaf of rye bread at the thriving kriegie flea market. Cigarettes were the currency of the POW camps. We then raffled the loaf, selling 1,200 tickets at one cigarette per ticket. With my share of six hundred cigarettes I purchased one of the very few fleece-lined leather flying jackets in the camp. I didn't realize what a vital role that jacket would play the following winter. Now, sixty years later, that jacket resides in a glass case in the RAF Elsham Wolds Association's memorial room, along with one of my three silk escape maps which the Germans never found.

On August 8, we were once more herded into the cattle cars for the second leg of our evacuation—a long nightmare journey of nearly five hundred miles, lasting three days. We subsisted on the food we brought with us; no meals were supplied. One or two unfortunate kriegies had lost their food on the march, and others shared with them. This was generous, but perhaps not as generous as it might seem since most of us found we had little appetite anyway due to the conditions we found ourselves in. And with no toilet facilities, we had all developed constipation.

A few times, when the train stopped long enough, we were allowed to get out and stretch our legs. We had to stay on one side of the train under the watchful eyes of vigilant guards. The guards on the other side of the train had orders to shoot on sight any POW foolish enough to venture there.

By the third day we traveled mostly in silence, except for the clacking of the wheels on the rails. Everyone was too benumbed to talk.

Finally we arrived at a station and were told to leave the train and take all our baggage with us. With this, we came alive and gave a cheer because we knew we had at last reached our destination.

Our new camp was Stamlager (or Stalag for short) 357 at Fallingbostel, some thirty miles south-southeast of Bremen. We liked this location because it was only about four hundred miles to the northeast of the British army which was battling its way from the French coast toward Belgium. It was comforting to know that we would be liberated by the British—not the Russians.

In no time at all the men in charge of the camp radio had it set up, and we began receiving daily news reports from London once again. Things were moving well on the Western Front; the optimists among us thought we would be home by Christmas.

The daylight raids by the U.S. Air Force were great morale boosters. Fallingbostel lay on one of the routes the planes took when bombing targets in central and eastern Germany. When the air raid sirens sounded we went outside and listened to the roar of the approaching bombers. We then lay on our backs and gazed in wonder at the great armada of hundreds of Flying Fortresses passing overhead in perfect formation at fifteen thousand feet. In every direction, as far as we could see, these great silver "birds" proclaimed the Allies' mastery of the skies over the German hinterland.

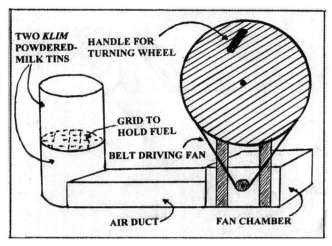

*A diagram of our "blower," the outdoor cooker we used at Fallingbostel. No hot food or drink if it was raining!*

By mid-1944 the Germans had withdrawn their antiaircraft guns and fighters from the countryside to concentrate them in defense of the cities. So the Allied formations were undisturbed as they flew overhead. However, at the target area it was different, and when we watched the planes on their return journey, we could see gaps in the formations showing where bombers had been shot down.

Because we would cheer as the Flying Fortresses flew over the camp, after several raids our captors ordered us to remain in our barracks when the sirens sounded. This was for our safety—so they said! We would crowd around the windows where we could still see some of the bombers.

The preparation of meals at Fallingbostel was quite different from other POW camps I had been in. I wrote the following in a letter to my parents on September 29, 1944: "Since leaving Stalag 6 we no longer have communal cooking but do our own on the most ingenious cooking contraption I have ever seen. But I must close now. In perfect health, John." (I had come to the end of the letter space on the page and didn't have room to continue to describe the cooking arrangements. But I did so later in a follow-up letter.)

At other camps the food in the Red Cross parcels was taken out and prepared by the camp cooks. But at Fallingbostel the cookhouse prepared only the meager rations supplied by the Germans—potatoes and sometimes turnips. Here we received Red Cross parcels intact and prepared any hot food or drink from these parcels ourselves on a homemade cooking device we called a "blower." I believe I can best explain it with my diagram on page 157. In a follow-up card to my parents I wrote:

Dear Mops & Dad,

I will now deal with the "blower" in this card. It is a cooking fire, with a forced draft. This is supplied by an air pipe. In this air pipe is situated a fan which is driven round at a colossal rate, with high gearing, by a big wheel turned by hand. The wheel drives the fan with a boot lace as a belt. Understand? I thought you would—not!

Cheerio, John.

The incredibly efficient "blower" could boil a can of water in a minute or two using only a few pieces of a cardboard box for fuel.

At Fallingbostel, like at Heydekrug, we formed combines consisting usually of four kriegies, though some combines had only two men, while others had as many as eight. The men in these combines pooled food items such as canned meat, cheese, tea, and coffee. This way we were able to vary the daily meal by opening a different can of meat each day. Each combine had its own blower.

# BLEAK WINTER TURNS TO JOY

For the first two months at Fallingbostel we received full food parcels each week. But by late September parcels stopped arriving. As the camp stock of food parcels dwindled, each man was issued half a parcel each week. The next week it was one parcel shared between four men. The following week eight men shared one parcel. The final issue, in mid-October, was one parcel divided between sixteen men.

In a card to Barbara, my younger sister, dated October 30, 1944, I wrote: "How about shaking up the Red Cross and get them to dump a few food parcels around this part of Germany? Today I ran out of my last reserves. Cheerio, Sis. Love, John."

At the time I wrote that card, we didn't realize that the reason the parcels had stopped coming was that the Allied air forces were wreaking havoc on the German railway system. Authorities used the few trains that could still run for transporting troops and ammunition, not for POW food parcels. However, some personal parcels still came through. On October 30 I wrote to my parents:

Dear Mops & Dad,
I have received three cigarette parcels just lately, thank goodness, as there is no food and very few cigarettes in the camp. Red Cross parcels ran out sometime ago. It is also quite cold and very damp, so our position here is not very bright at the moment. I have had to tighten up my belt a bit.

Our daily calorie intake dropped drastically—from around twenty-three hundred to about three hundred—now that we were depending almost entirely on the inadequate German rations. In a short four-week period, life in camp took a dramatic turn. All sporting activity stopped, as did walking around the compound for exercise. As the weeks passed and we got weaker from malnutrition, and the cold winter winds started to blow through the many cracks of the raised wooden floor, we huddled miserably on our bunks, dreading the whistle announcing time for appel.

Jack Mason, Eric Spong, and I were still together; we had saved a little food for Christmas. When December 25 arrived we hungrily prepared a special meal. But that was a mistake. Our stomachs had shrunk so much, they rebelled against this unaccustomed quantity and richness. Not wanting to vomit and waste this precious food, we lay on our bunks in considerable discomfort.

Spong and I shared a double bunk; he had the lower and I the upper. As the nights grew colder, we would lie shivering as we tried to sleep. One evening Eric and I decided to double-up in one bunk, sleeping head-to-toe. There wasn't much room, and occasionally we would poke each other in the face with our feet, but this way we were able to keep reasonably warm with double the blankets and shared body heat.

As the winter progressed, with its misery of deprivation and a cold that penetrated to our very bones, we spent the days curled up on our bunks. Only the shrill whistle calling us to appel and the arrival of the thin, watery potato soup would drag us from the cover of our blankets. As we lined up at appel for the count, I was envied, as I stood wearing my fleece-lined flying jacket. I don't know how I would have coped that winter without it.

About this time my eyesight became blurred so that I could recognize people only when I was close to them. Shortly after my eye trouble began, I started having a problem walking. Everyone was walking slowly because of undernourishment, but now, if I bumped my foot against even a small object, I would stumble and sometimes fall. Then I realized I had little, or no, feeling in my legs below the knees. When I pricked my calf muscles with a pin, I couldn't feel it.

## BLEAK WINTER TURNS TO JOY

Was I alarmed by these developments? Along with malnutrition and the constant cold, had come a pervasive spirit of apathy. I regarded my physical problems with resignation rather than alarm.

But there was one event that kept our morale high—the evening news reports from our clandestine radio. We would softly cheer as we learned of Allied advances on the different fronts, and for a short while there would be animated discussions about how soon the war would end.

Slowly that grim winter gave way to spring. The warming sunshine gradually dispelled the cold that had caused so much hardship. The German rations improved a little; now we occasionally received sauerkraut and the small round cheeses that in earlier days we had considered so awful that we buried them. Now we hungrily devoured them.

Hitler's vaunted Third Reich was crumbling rapidly. Gone was his dream that it would last for a thousand years. The Allied spring offensives were underway. Life came back into the camp, and our spirits soared. As March came to a close the British and Canadian armies, that had liberated Holland, were poised to invade Germany itself. Field Marshal Montgomery's Armored Corp was only about seventy miles away. An air of excitement pervaded Fallingbostel POW camp as we speculated that the Brits would reach us in less than two weeks.

Then, on April 4, the Germans dropped a bombshell. They informed us that the camp was going to be evacuated and that we had two days to get ready for the march east, away from the advancing British army! For me, in my physical condition, such a march would spell disaster. I would not be able to keep up with the march and could be shot as a straggler. I tried to be admitted to the sickbay that would remain at the camp. The British medical officer didn't think my condition warranted admitting me.

When I talked to Jack Mason about it, he said, "John, you've got to escape."

"Escape! Jack, what on earth are you talking about? How can I escape from this place in my condition?"

"John, I have an idea. You know the barrack near the gate? That's the one barrack we can hide under when the camp is evacuated."

As I thought about it, my heart filled with hope. "You're right, Jack," I exclaimed excitedly.

All the barracks were built with floors raised about two feet above the ground. This prevented tunnels being built since the ferrets could look underneath. However, the barrack near the gate was different. It was occupied by the kriegies who worked in the German forlager performing duties that helped the camp to run smoothly. But the Germans required them to sign parole, which meant, according to international law, that they could not try to escape. Because of this they were allowed to bank up earth around their barrack preventing the cold winter wind from blowing through the wide cracks between the floorboards.

After explaining our plan to the occupants, they were cooperative, however, they thought we were crazy. "The war is about to end," they cautioned us. "Why take the risk?"

Our plan was to dig a shallow pit under the floor, just big enough for us to lie in. Since we had only two days, we began immediately.

First we pried a few floorboards loose so we could get under the floor. While we were digging, the occupants replaced the floorboards and kept watch. They tapped on the floor to warn us of the presence of goons.

Because of our weakened condition we worked slowly, but before the end of the second day we had completed the digging. The men who lived in this barrack kindly gave us enough bed boards to cover the pit. We left a small gap at one end through which we could wriggle feet first, one at a time. Lastly, we covered the bed boards with some of the excavated dirt, spreading the rest around, just in case the goons checked underneath the floor with a flashlight.

The next morning the evacuation began, starting with the barracks farthest from the gate. With five thousand kriegies, the evacuation took several hours. As the line of guards moved closer to the gate, Mason and I got down into our pit. The other men wished us luck. One of them said, "I still think you're crazy. What if the Germans set fire to the barracks so the Brits can't use them?"

Jack replied, "We'll take our chance on that. We'll be back in Old Blighty¹ while you're still wandering around Germany." This turned out to be an accurate prophecy.

After the men replaced the floorboards, we heard them dragging a table and chairs to cover the area.

As we lay in the pit, we could hear shouting and the sound of hundreds of marching feet on the road barely thirty feet away. About an hour later, these sounds slowly receded as the end of the long marching column moved farther away from the camp. Then it became eerily silent. We strained our ears, listening intently for the crackling sound of fire above us. But as the silence continued, we began to relax.

We waited maybe another hour, talking only in whispers. Finally we wriggled our way out of the pit and to the side of the barrack facing the gate. Cautiously we scraped away some of the dirt and peered out. The camp was deserted except for a few kriegies standing near the open gate. They were orderlies who worked in the sickbay. Believing we were in no danger now of being apprehended, we enlarged the hole and crawled out. When the orderlies saw us, their mouths fell open. One asked, "Where did you chaps come from?"

As we dusted the dirt off our uniforms, Mason explained how we had hidden. We then enquired about any German guards. We learned that several goons had remained behind as token guards of the camp. But in the days that followed we saw very little of them, and they left us alone.

Mason and I decided that the safest thing to do would be to remain in the camp and wait for either the British or the Canadian army to arrive. It would be one or the other, we were sure. But food was the big question. Certainly the evacuated kriegies would not have left any behind. Mason said he was going to look around the German compound. Worn out by the exertion of the past two days, I let him go on his foraging trip by himself while I sat on the steps of the barrack, enjoying the warm spring sunshine. Maybe it was my high rate of metabolism that led to my physical problems when the Red Cross food supplies dried up. Mason and the other men fared a lot better that I did.

*Our dream comes true! British tanks in the German hinterland.*

After a while Mason returned with a broad smile on his face and his arms full of food—a loaf of rye bread, several cans of meat, sauerkraut, and margarine. In one of the buildings he had found a large supply of food the Germans had not been able to take with them on the march. He reported that he had seen a couple of goons, but they took no notice of him. Knowing that in a few days they themselves would become POWs, they weren't going to antagonize the few kriegies in the camp. It was funny to see some of them still manning some of the goon boxes. However, they didn't guard the gate, and we could wander in and out at will.

For the first time in months we were able to start eating adequately again. But we were careful not to eat too much too quickly. That wasn't difficult; we had been deprived of proper meals for so long that our stomachs weren't ready for a large quantity of food at one time. We remembered our mistake at Christmas when we had foolishly gorged. But it wasn't long until we were satisfying our ravenous hunger with three hearty meals a day. Slowly I began to feel stronger; my eyesight started to improve. But it would be two or three months before I would be able to run.

With every new day came the hope and anticipation that the British army would arrive that day. One sunny morning—April 16, 1945—I was lounging on the barracks steps while Mason was chatting with two or three men near the gate. Suddenly they all became very excited and started pointing. Jack called out to me, "John, come quickly! It's Monty's mob! It's Monty's mob! It's Monty's mob!" He was beside himself with excitement, as were the other men. He was referring, of course, to the British army commanded by Field Marshal Bernard Montgomery.

Gazing down the hillside, I first I saw a cloud of dust, and then, in front of the dust, I was able to make out a long line of camouflaged tanks roaring eastward across the valley. Not knowing whether to laugh or cry, I said, "Jack, we've made it. We've finally made it!" For a few moments we looked into each other's eyes, and then our arms were around each other, and we were locked in a tight embrace.

For me it was "third time lucky!"

Then I heard the sound of deep sobbing. Looking back to the fence, I saw Georgie Booth holding the barbed wire with both hands, his thin frame shaking with every sob. On September 4, 1939, only three days after the war in Europe had started, Booth and Larry Slattery had been shot down while on a bombing mission against Wilhelmshaven. Their POW numbers were "1"and "2." They had been POWs for 2,051 days! Both Booth and Slattery had been in the sickbay when the camp had been evacuated. As we gathered around him, one of the men put his arms around his shaking shoulders.

We all had tears of joy in our eyes, and soon we were all talking excitedly at the same time. We had been waiting for this day since we were first captured and had heard those fateful words, "For you, the war is over."

Before long we noticed that all the German guards had disappeared. Our curiosity aroused, one of the orderlies checked the administrative building and found the guards had locked themselves inside the guardroom. We laughed, thinking it funny—and satisfying—that our captors had made themselves captives in anticipation of the Brits taking over the camp!

We didn't have long to wait for the British army to reach the camp. Early in the afternoon, the quietness was broken by the sound of an approaching vehicle. Quickly, about a dozen of us gathered at the open gate in time to watch a camouflaged armored car rolling across the administrative compound toward us. It stopped just fifteen feet away.

We stood in spellbound silence as the hatch was thrown open and the head of a grimy-faced soldier appeared, wearing a Scottish beret. Looking at us, he said in a broad Scottish brogue, "Men, you are now liberated!" Only then was the spell broken. Yelling in uncontrolled excitement, we ran to the vehicle, touching it almost in disbelief as the two soldiers climbed out. The emotion of that moment was indescribable. Tears ran down the cheeks of Georgie Booth. Even now, nearly sixty years later, the memory of that longed-for moment sends shivers down my back!

We crowded around the soldiers, laughing, shaking their hands, slapping their backs, and all of us asking questions at the same time. The corporal in charge raised his hands and pleaded, "One at a time, men."

As we quieted down, someone asked, "What's your outfit, Jock?"

"Eleventh Hussars, Seventh Armored Division."

"How much longer is the war going to last?"

"It's almost over. We'll soon be shaking hands with the Ruskies."

---

[1] A nickname for England.

# FREE AT LAST!

The next morning Mason, who was in amazingly good shape, told me he was going to explore the area where the camp was located. Hours later he came back with a rifle slung across his back, and wheeling two bicycles.

"Jack, whatever have you been up to?" I asked.

Grinning, he replied, "Just relieving the Jerries of a little of their unnecessary hardware. With these we won't have to stay in the camp. We can scout around a bit."

"I hope I can cope with riding a bike," I replied.

The next day we headed out into the countryside. I was a bit slow, but it was great to be out on the road without fear of being captured by an enemy. While passing a farm Mason saw a motorcycle parked outside. "Stop, John," he said. "I think we're going to do a little swap!"

The German farmer eyed us warily as we pedaled into the yard and dismounted. With his hand resting on the butt of the rifle slung across his back, Mason said, *"Wir waren Kriegsgefangene."* ("We were prisoners of war.") Seeing a look of apprehension come over the farmer's face, Mason continued, *"Wir sind Englisch."* ("We are English.")

The fear left his face when he heard we were British. He had thought we might be Russian POWs whom the Germans had treated so terribly. It is estimated that over thirty thousand Russian POWs died during the war in that part of Germany. The civilians were now fearful of reprisals. However, the farmer was not happy when he learned we were going to trade our two bicycles for his motorcycle.

For a few days we roamed far and wide, enjoying our newfound freedom. I sat behind Mason with the rifle slung across my back. On one occasion we went right up to the front where we were able to get a close view of the mechanized equipment our army had. As we passed alongside scores of stationary tanks, we saw one that had a long steel boom anchored on top with a lot of thick chains hanging from its end. The soldiers told us that when they came to a mine field, this tank flailed the ground to detonate the mines, thus clearing a narrow passage for the rest of the tanks to pass through. Another unusual-looking tank carried a steel bridge that it could lay across narrow, but deep, waterways. After the rest of the column had passed over the bridge, the tank would pick it up for future use. In this way the rapid advance of the column was not slowed down by narrow, difficult water obstacles.

At this time we got some terrible reports from the notorious Belsen concentration camp, located about fifty or sixty miles to the south. Since he had the motorbike, Mason decided to go there to check out these gruesome reports. I was still getting tired quickly so I decided not to go with him. I wish now that I had. He returned with a horrifying report of a large pile made up of hundreds of human corpses. The bodies were literally just skin and bones. Only people who had been slowly starved over a long period of time could have been reduced to that state before eventually dying. Mason said that he went through the commandant's house, later known as "the Beast of Belsen." He reported seeing a table lamp, the shade of which had been made out of human skin.

A few weeks later, I sat in a cinema in England and watched a newsreel report of the Belsen concentration camp. It confirmed everything Mason had told me—and worse. World War II was indeed a righteous war to rid the world of a horrendous evil.

By April 20 the British Military Government was established in northwest Germany, and Mason and I were required to turn in the motorcycle and the rifle. The camp was rapidly filling with other liberated servicemen, including a lot of lower-ranking men who had been working on German farms and other projects. The British established an administration to run the camp, supply meals, and maintain a reasonable level of military discipline. We were no longer allowed to wander around the countryside, and there was a lot of grumbling about the delay in our repatriation to England.

Finally, on April 26, 1945, Mason and I were in the first large batch of two or three hundred ex-POWs transported in a convoy to an airfield in Holland. After the convoy had parked along two sides of a large open area, an announcement over a loudspeaker instructed any officers to report to the administra-tion building. I climbed out of my truck, shook hands with Jack Mason, and sadly said Goodbye. It would be fourteen years before I would see him again. I walked with three or four other officers across the open area, accompanied by catcalls and whistles. It was the men's last chance to openly jeer at an officer!

In less than two hours I was gazing down on the English coast that I had last flown over that fateful night twenty-five months earlier. The transport plane landed at Cosford, one of the RAF stations that had been set up to process the thousands of RAF ex-POWs who would soon be lib-erated and repatriated.

*This photo of me was taken shortly after the end of the war in Europe.*

After identification, we underwent de-lousing treatment and hot showers. All our clothing was scrapped, and we were completely reoutfitted. Our new battledress uniforms showed our rank, aircrew wings, and cam-paign medal ribbons. With accumulated seniority, I now had the rank of flight lieutenant (the RAF equivalent of captain). Next we had a thorough medical examination; mine showed I was fit enough to go home on leave. Only then could I go to the phone and dial that never-to-be-forgotten phone number—Ruislip 2549.

I gripped the phone tightly and pressed it against my ear. It had been such a long time since I had heard that dear voice say, "Hello."

Controlling my emotions I said, "Dad, this is John. I'm back in England."

"John, my son!" my father exclaimed. Then I heard him call out, "Ethel, come quickly. John is on the phone!"

A moment later I heard my mother say, "John, my darling boy, is it really you?"

"Yes, Mops. I arrived back this afternoon. I escaped from the Germans three weeks ago when they evacuated our camp. That's why I got back to England early." The war had not yet ended, and my parents were still wondering whether, in the turmoil of Germany's final collapse, I was safe and where I was.

I continued, "I'll be coming home on leave the day after tomorrow. I'll phone you again when I get to London."

When I reached London and phoned home, my father told me he would meet me at the suburban train station in Ruislip, a nearby town. From there our local bus would take us to the end of our road. This would save me walking one mile from the Ickenham station. My father didn't have a car.

I was slowly walking to the footbridge over the railway tracks at Ruislip station, when I saw my father hurry onto the other platform. We met in the center of the footbridge, and in a moment we were locked in a tight, lingering embrace.

Releasing me, Dad said, "If we hurry we can catch the bus before it leaves."

"Dad, I can't hurry."

Giving me a quick look of concern, he said, "I'll hold the bus." And he ran back to the bus stop.

Arriving at the bus, I handed my kitbag up to my father. Then with both hands I lifted one leg onto the first step and, grasping the two handrails, I pulled myself up into the bus. I heard my father tell the other passengers, "This is my son. He has just got back from the prisoner of war camp." There was spontaneous clapping as I pulled myself up the second step and sat down.

As the bus left Ruislip station and turned along the road leading to Ickenham, I feasted my eyes on the old familiar landmarks. In less than fifteen minutes we reached the village. My heart beat faster as once again I saw the ancient, historic church, the old pub with its original stables, the pond, and the tall, ornate village pump under its large, sturdy gazebo. I remembered how that old gazebo had been sandbagged back in 1940, during the threat of a German invasion, and how, two nights a week, I had stood guard there when I was still only sixteen. I had been the only boy in our village Home Guard unit.

A mile from the village center the bus stopped to let Dad and me get off. My Dad carried my kitbag as I tried to hurry down the road. And then I was gazing at our house, "St. Ives," with its gabled porch, lead-paned windows, and the cream-colored climbing rose covering the wall. Home at last! A lingering embrace with my tearful mother, a lot of talking, and a wonderful dinner—what a fantastic welcome home I received. It was euphoric!

After nine days, during which time I did little more than eat, lay around, and sleep late, the war was finally over. May 8, 1945, was proclaimed VE (Victory Europe) Day.

I decided to celebrate this momentous occasion in London, the city in which my father had worked in banking for forty years; the city which had given its name to my school, the City of London School; the city which had suffered so much in the 1940 German blitzing. My train to Piccadilly Circus soon became crowded with jubilant passengers. No one was a stranger; everyone talked to whomever was close. Because I was in uniform, I received many handshakes, backslaps, and warm commendations. In the spirit of the time, all military personnel were being treated as heroes.

Arriving at Piccadilly Circus, I joined the rapidly growing crowds. Everywhere happy people were laughing and singing. Someone shouted, "Let's go to Buckingham Palace." At once many of us started to move, first to Trafalgar Square, then under Admiralty Arch, and finally along the Mall to Buckingham Palace.

As we crowded around the Victoria Monument in front of the palace, we started chanting in unison, "We want the king! We want the king!" We continued this chant until King George and Queen Elizabeth appeared on the palace balcony, at which time a thunderous roar of victory went up from the jubilant crowd. Everywhere, the atmosphere was one of triumphant exhilaration.

*Picadilly Circus, VE Day, 1945*

*VE Day, 1945, outside Buckingham Palace*

I was sure Jack Mason, a Londoner, was also somewhere out in the crowds. I remembered his words to those kriegies who thought we were crazy when we got down into our hideaway pit—"We'll be back in Old Blighty while you're still wandering around Germany." I wondered about those five thousand men. What had happened to them after they marched away from Falingbostel?

It was nearly twenty years later before I found out.

I was reading *The Fall of Berlin* by David Fisher. In one chapter, the author deviated from the general theme of the book to relate a tragedy which came very close to becoming a major disaster for Britain and the Commonwealth countries. In the fading light one evening just a few days before the end of the war, an RAF patrol of two tank-busting Typhoons mistook a large column of POWs for a column of German soldiers and attacked it with cannon fire and rockets. Sixty airmen were killed and many others wounded. British Intelligence had no knowledge of POWs being out in the countryside.

The author went on to relate how the British camp leader and secretary immediately approached Oberst (Colonel) Ostmann, the German commandant. The author named them—Dixie Dean and Ron Mogg. As soon as I read those two names, I knew David Fisher was writing about the POWs from Fallingbostel. Dixie Dean told the commandant that somehow a message had to be gotten through to the RAF before dawn, otherwise disaster would overtake them with an all-out attack by the whole squadron. He demanded two bicycles, one for himself and one for a German escort, and also some papers of identification. Only after threats of dire consequences to him personally, did Oberst Ostmann acquiesce.

Dean and the German guard cycled throughout the night in the general direction of the British positions. As dawn was breaking they providentially ran into a British army patrol. At first the Tommies wanted to treat Dean as an enemy along with the German guard, but with his authoritative personality, Dean persuaded them to hurry him to their commanding officer.

Quickly Dean explained what had happened. The officer grabbed his radio field telephone and in seconds was talking to the RAF commanding officer. The whole squadron of Typhoons was already on the runway, awaiting the order to take off when the strike was abruptly cancelled. Dixie Dean had made it through the night just in time. Yes, the "friendly fire" of the previous evening had been a tragedy, but a terrible disaster of far greater magnitude had been averted with only a minute to spare!

In mid-May my leave ended, and I received instructions to report to the RAF Rehabilitation Center for ex-POWs, located in East Anglia. I was full of hope that I would soon be back in a squadron. On the first or second day at the rehabilitation center, we were told to gather at the edge of the airfield for a display by the RAF's most advanced fighter. The officer pointed across the airfield to where the plane would appear. He told us to watch carefully and that the plane would be flying low, at about two hundred feet.

"Look, men. There it comes," the officer called out.

We heard a loud whine, then a roar unlike the sound of any other plane we had known. No sooner had we focused on the plane than it was over our heads and disappearing behind us into the distance.

"What on earth was that?" someone exclaimed, as the rest of us stood with our mouths open in awe and amazement.

Smiling, the officer explained it was a twin-engine Gloster Meteor, the RAF's first jet fighter. It had been put into service against the Germans in July 1944. We learned it could reach the unheard-of speed of almost five hundred miles per hour at thirty thousand feet. By the end of the war in Europe, about two hundred had been produced. The officer raised another gasp of wonder from the admiring ex-kriegies when he casually mentioned that the jet had flown over us on only one engine. This display of British inventive prowess made us all the keener to get back into flying.

But now it was time for the stringent physical examination required for airmen, with special attention being given to eyesight. I was told that my eyesight had been permanently impaired while a POW, and that this disqualified me for flying. Within a year I was wearing glasses. I was offered the position as Assistant Transportation Officer at Southampton, which in no way appealed to me. I was bitterly disappointed!

# FREE AT LAST!

We were told we could apply for a variety of courses, at special Resettlement Centers, that would prepare us for college entrance. Alternatively, we could ask for immediate demobilization. If we chose a resettlement course we would be sent on indefinite leave with full pay until a place became available. I asked for a course that would prepare me for agricultural college. My indefinite leave lasted six-and-a-half months.

Returning home, I soon became bored with the long hours of inactivity. All my pre-war friends, except Geofrey Sones, were still in the armed forces and wouldn't be demobilized until 1946. Geof was diabetic and, therefore, had not been drafted. He worked with a construction company and helped me get a temporary job there while I waited for my resettlement course.

But as the months passed, my interests changed from agriculture to building construction. I decided to make building construction a career, specializing in reinforced concrete roofing. I started taking night classes on this subject. In December 1945, when told to report for the resettlement course, I asked for demobilization. I remained an officer in the RAF Reserve.

By the summer of 1946 I had become dissatisfied with the daily commuting back and forth to London. One Sunday, I was helping my father refasten the large climbing rose which had fallen away from the front of the house. "Dad," I said, "I can't stand spending three hours a day commuting back and forth into London. That's an eighth of a day, and I think it's such a waste of time. You've been doing it for forty years. Do you realize, Dad, you've spent a total of five years traveling in a train?"

After a while my father said, "John, Mr. Rushton, my friend up in the City [the center of London where my father worked] was telling me the other day that tea companies are now looking for young men to manage their plantations out in India. Do you think that kind of life would interest you?"

"You bet it would," I exclaimed. For the first time in months I felt a surge of enthusiasm.

"Why don't you write Mr. Rushton a letter? I'll give it to him."

That evening I wrote a letter. Ten weeks later I was on an ocean liner heading toward India and a new life.

# TIGERS, ELEPHANTS, AND WHISKEY

My seventeen-day journey to India was in stark contrast to the two ocean voyages I had made during the war. This postwar voyage was leisurely, with no fear of lurking submarines or deadly torpedoes. I basked under cloudless skies as the ship cruised at about twenty-eight knots[1] through the Mediterranean Sea. However, I welcomed the shade of the promenade deck as the ship slowly made its way through the Suez Canal to the Red Sea.

Sometimes in the summer, when the wind in the Red Sea was traveling in the same direction and at the same speed as a ship, it would become so unbearably hot that the ship would turn around and steam against the wind until it cooled down. Fortunately we did not experience such discomfort. It was cool and pleasant as we crossed the Arabian Sea toward mystical India, with its history as old as that of ancient Egypt.

The cultural shock I experienced when we arrived at Bombay was profound. The crowds, the noise, the bustle, and the beggars told me I had come to a different world! I would soon learn that India is a land of contrasts—inordinate filth and incredible beauty, languishing poverty and luxurious wealth, extreme ignorance (though often with innate wisdom) and extensive knowledge.

Whether one fell in love with India—and stayed—or tried to leave on the first available ship (now a plane) depended on one's attitude. After a thirty-six-hour train journey across India (about which the less said, the better!), I arrived in the vast city of Calcutta, where, years later, Mother Teresa carried out her noble ministry among the many homeless people she found dying alone on the streets. During my orientation at the Calcutta office of my company, the British CEO spoke about another cultural difference I would face—the speed, or lack of it, at which things got done. There was always *"Tora pichhi hoga."* ("In a little while.") "Curnow," he said, "if you plan to stay in India, remember this ditty: 'Here lie the bones of our dear deceased, who tried to hurry the unhurrying East.' "

The last leg of my journey was an overnight train trip, north from Calcutta through what is now Bangladesh. The following morning, toward the end of the journey, the train entered the tea growing area of North Bengal. For the first time I was looking at tea plantations. The tea bushes, planted three feet apart and pruned to a height of thirty-four inches, formed a carpet of green stretching over hundreds of acres. Tall shade trees, in neat rows forty feet apart, enhanced the scenic landscape.

At about 10 A.M. the train pulled into Dalsingpara station at the end of the railway line. Just three or four miles north lay the international frontier with the kingdom of Bhutan, where the foothills of the Himalayan mountains rose sharply from the plains of Bengal. Dalsingpara Tea Estate would be my home for the next seven years. It was one of nine tea estates owned by the Nedeem Tea Company.

As I climbed down from the train I was glad to see Bobby Toms, the Scottish manager, there to meet me. Several Indians looked at me with curiosity. There had not been a young assistant manager on the plantation since 1939 when the war began.

After a railway worker had loaded my bags into Toms's car, we headed toward the factory compound and his house. I was all eyes as I looked around at the many new, and sometimes strange, sights. As we neared the factory a *babu* (an English-speaking Bengali clerk) waved us down.

"Sir, a tiger has killed a cow on the road to Toorsa [a smaller Nedeem Company plantation sandwiched between Dalsinpara and Bhutan]. They want you to come and shoot the tiger," the babu told Toms excitedly.

"Can a *macchan* [tree platform] be built nearby?" Toms asked.

"A *macchan* has already been made. The kill is lying at the edge of the road next to some jungle."

"What time should I be there?"

"Not any later than four o'clock, Sir."

"I'll be there," Toms assured the *babu* as we drove off.

"Well, how about that, Curnow. Your first day on the plantation, and there's a tiger kill. Do you want to come? It can be dangerous, you know."

"I wouldn't miss it for the world," I replied.

"Do you have a gun?"

"I have a shotgun, but I don't have a big game rifle."

"No matter," Toms said.

Mrs. Toms, a pleasant Scottish lady, showed me to the room I would occupy for the next two or three days, before moving into my own bungalow. "The *paniwallah* [water boy] has your bath ready. Lunch will be at twelve-thirty," she said, smiling.

Shortly before four in the afternoon we drove toward Toorsa. About half way along the dirt road two men signaled us to stop. The dead cow was lying by the right side of the road. The men pointed to a small tree at the edge of the jungle on the left side of the road. The *macchan,* about four feet square and twelve or thirteen feet off the ground, was well hidden by the leaves of the tree. It was about thirty feet from the kill.

The men helped us climb onto the platform and handed Toms his double-barreled hunting rifle. Toms told the driver to come back in a couple of hours. Toms and I squatted on the platform at right angles to each other, so that he was facing the kill, and I would be able to see the tiger if it came out of the jungle.

As we settled down to wait, Toms reminded me that it was imperative we maintain absolute silence. "If the tiger comes from your side, give a little nudge with your elbow. If I see it, I'll give you a nudge," he said as he cocked his rifle.

The minutes passed as the sun slowly dropped and the shadows lengthened. After about twenty minutes I felt a gentle nudge. Very slowly I turned my head to look across the road. A huge tiger was sitting a few feet from its kill. Since it was facing us, its massive head and chest presented Toms with a perfect target. Slowly he lifted the rifle and, taking aim, squeezed the trigger. His shoulder jerked back against me from the recoil of the powerful rifle. The tiger gave a shattering roar and leapt upward. But instead of falling back dead, it charged off into the scrub.

"This is serious," Toms muttered, as he signaled for silence. We strained our ears for the slightest sound that would indicate the animal was somewhere nearby. After several minutes of total silence we climbed down to examine the ground for signs of blood. There were none. Apparently Toms had missed completely. He was relieved that he hadn't wounded the tiger. He explained that a wounded tiger is extremely dangerous. Disabled and unable to catch its natural prey, the tiger would be driven by hunger to overcome its instinctive fear of human beings and become a man eater. Wounded tigers or leopards had to be hunted down and killed before there was any loss of human life.

I was amazed that Toms had missed such a large target at such close range. At rifle practice in the RAF, our target on the twenty-five-yard range was only about six inches square, with the bull's eye one inch in diameter. If we didn't get a bull's eye, we certainly hit the target. And here the tiger was only about ten yards away.

I had arrived on Saturday, which was the day the local club had its weekly meeting. Its membership consisted of the British managerial staffs of the local tea estates that made up the district. Tennis occupied the afternoon hours, while the evening was spent socializing, Scotch whisky being the favorite beverage. Later that evening, after the tiger "fiasco," Bobby Toms and his wife took me to the club, where I met the other members. One of them was Gordon Fraser, whose left arm was withered. He was the manager of the Toorsa plantation.

After Toms related our earlier experience with the tiger, he said, "Fraser, tell Curnow about your arm."

We sat around, sipping our whiskies, as Fraser told his story.

He, with several other tea planters, had been on an organized hunt. Indian coolies, beating through the jungle, drove the game into an open area where the hunters, riding on elephants, were waiting.

Suddenly a large tiger broke out of the jungle, and, seeing its way barred by Fraser, charged. Before Fraser could take aim, the tiger sprang, knocking him off his elephant's back. Remaining calm, the *mahout* (elephant driver) wheeled the elephant around, whereupon it crushed the tiger to death with one of its huge front feet. But not before the big cat had badly mauled Fraser's arm.

"You mean to say a tiger can spring that high?" I asked.

"Listen, Curnow," one of the other men said. "A tiger once raided a stockade and killed a small cow. Holding the cow in its jaws by the neck, and with the body slung over its back, it cleared the eight-foot-high stockade fence and got away with its kill. You don't mess with tigers. They're strong animals."

I thought how Toms and I had been sitting only about twelve feet off the ground.

The following Monday evening Toms took me to the club of the Kalchini District, about thirteen miles away. This club showed movies every Monday evening. One of the men there walked with a pronounced limp. I learned he had been sitting in a *macchan* with another tea planter, waiting for a tiger to return to its kill. The angered tiger saw them, sprang onto the *macchan,* and dragged him to the ground. Only a good shot by his friend saved him from being killed. As it was, his badly mauled left leg had to be amputated below the knee.

I now found myself viewing tiger hunting in a new light. I understood that Toms may have missed the tiger because of nervousness, since our *macchan* was low enough for a tiger to reach it. If there had been a suitable taller tree nearby, the platform would have been constructed at a higher level. A few years later, Stan Spriggens, the assistant manager of Toorsa, shot a very large tiger measuring thirteen feet from its nose to the tip of its tail. It set a district record. It was believed that this was the same tiger Toms missed.

The tiger I saw on my first day at Dalsingpara was the only live one, living in the wild, that I saw during my twenty-seven years in India.

A few weeks following the incident with Toms and the tiger the government Forest Department decided to hold a *kedhah* to capture some wild elephants to be tamed and trained as work animals. We were invited to the roundup.

A round stockade, forty feet in diameter and made of ten- to twelve-inch tree trunks, was built deep in the jungle. The heavy gate was suspended like a trapdoor so that it could be dropped quickly, and a long funnel, narrowing to the width of the gate at the stockade was constructed through the jungle. When everything was ready and a herd of elephants had been located, hundreds of Indian coolies, in a large semicircle, slowly advanced through the jungle, beating on drums and metal objects and maneuvering the elephants down the funnel and into the stockade. Then the heavy gate was quickly dropped into position. Once the elephants realized they were trapped they began screaming. The noise was deafening. We usually think of elephants trumpeting, but these animals were screaming rather than trumpeting.

A huge bull, six or seven cows, and a couple of calves had been captured. The bull began to lunge at the stockade wall. Fortunately he had no room to pick up speed and momentum and, though the thick tree trunks creaked, they were able to withstand his lunges.

These experiences formed my introduction to India. I would live there for twenty-seven years and fall in love with the country and its people.

---

[1] One knot equals one nautical mile (6,080 feet) traveled in one hour. One nautical mile equals 1.15 land miles. Sixty nautical miles equals one degree of longitude at the equator. This measure is used in navigation.

# BECOMING A TEA MAKER

My first job as a new assistant manager for the tea estate was to learn Hindustani. Most of the eighteen hundred workers belonged to four main tribal groups—the Mundas, the Kurias, the Oraons, and the Santalis. In addition, Dalsingpara had a large group of workers originating from Nepal. Each group spoke a different language. However, everyone was bilingual, speaking Hindustani as well as their native language. After about three or four months I was able to communicate fairly well in Hindustani. However, I still had to translate everything in my head first. It was only after about a year that I was able to speak Hindustani fluently and not have to go though the mental translation process.

In addition to the labor force there was a clerical staff, made up almost entirely of educated Bengalis who spoke English as a second language.

I soon came to love the work and the laborers. They were simple folk with simple needs and lifestyles. They trusted the foreign *sahib* (literally "lord" or "master"), and it was a challenge to balance their interests with those of the company. As time went on and my managerial influence increased, I learned that the laborers had given me a nickname: the *Sidhah Sahib* (the Straight Master). I was proud of that nickname and endeavored to live up to it.

Being a new assistant manager meant hands-on learning. I had to learn how to propagate, grow, and maintain the health of the tea bushes. I also had to learn the manufacturing process carried out in the factory where the fresh green leaves from the plantation were transformed into dry black tea. I had to master the art of maintaining a reasonably high standard of work from the workers. Common sense, fairness, and a sense of humor were important ingredients for maintaining a good relationship with the labor force. This was especially important in the wet, hot plucking season when as much as 135 inches of rain fell in three-and-a-half months and the temperature could soar to above 100 degrees Fahrenheit, with the humidity at 100 percent! Tempers could become short under these conditions.

*New tea acreage. Seedlings, 1953.*

*New tea acreage. Mature bushes, 1958. Charlie Rutherford, John, and Joan.*

*New tea acreage. Close-up of bushes, 1958.*

Dalsingpara was a large plantation of some 4,000 acres, 1,350 of which were under tea cultivation. The remaining acreage was taken up by the factory area, housing, thatch and bamboo (used for building housing for the laborers), grazing land for cattle, and virgin jungle. Before leaving Dalsingpara seven-and-a-half years later, I converted 120 acres of jungle into new tea.

Britain still ruled India at this time, and all the British tea planters were members of the North Bengal Mounted Rifles (NBMR), a paramilitary organization sponsored by the British government. We were issued rifles and received an allowance to cover the expenses of maintaining a horse.

On August 15, 1947, Britain finally granted independence to India. Shortly afterward, the new Indian government disbanded the NBMR, along with all other similar paramilitary groups, collected the rifles, and terminated the horse allowance. Since I couldn't afford to maintain a horse without the government subsidy, I reluctantly sold it to an Indian merchant.

The transition to independence on the Indian subcontinent was traumatic, and in two areas there was terrible communal violence between Hindus and Moslems with heavy loss of life. Independence brought about partition, with the new Islamic country of West and East Pakistan being carved from the predominantly Hindu subcontinent. East Pakistan was created by dividing Bengal, which was on the east side of India. The part of Bengal remaining in India was renamed West Bengal. The state of Assam and the northeastern territories of Tripura, Manipur, and Nagaland remained connected to the main part of India by a long, narrow strip of West Bengal, stretching along the base of the Himalayan foothills and adjacent to the country of Bhutan. Dalsingpara was located in this narrow strip, as were many other British-owned tea plantations.

Plans were made to evacuate British women and children should the need arise. In the weeks before independence, the NBMR was mobilized and exercises were carried out so that we would be ready to quickly man roadblocks and secure bridges on the main east-west highway. Armed escorts were organized for the convoys that would take the women and children to two or three guarded airstrips. It was a time of considerable uncertainty and some apprehension. No one knew what the outcome would be as nearly three hundred and fifty years of British control came to an end.

# BECOMING A TEA MAKER

As it turned out, the transition of power was peaceful in our part of Bengal; frequently Indians would shake our hands and thank us for giving independence to their country.

Further to the south the situation was tragically different. Thousands of people—men, women, and children—were massacred including Hindus, as they fled to India from the newly created East Pakistan, and Moslems, as they fled from the Indian portion of Bengal to East Pakistan. On the West Pakistan side, where the state of Punjab was divided, the situation was even worse. Trains crowded with refugees, fleeing either east or west, were stopped by murderous gangs of either Moslems or Hindus and all the helpless passengers slaughtered. If my memory is correct, as many as half a million people died—perhaps more. It was months before things settled down, but the animosity created at that time between the two countries remains to this day.

Five-and-a-half months later, on January 30, 1948, tragedy struck the fledgling, independent, country of India when Mahatma[1] Gandhi was assassinated by Nathuran Godsey, a Hindu fanatic. This tragedy not only put India into deep mourning, but was considered an international catastrophe worldwide. Gandhi had become the revered international symbol of nonviolence and a free India; his country reeled under the shock of his murder.

In the spring of the following year, Bobby Toms and his wife returned to the U.K. on furlough, and Jack Edge, the manager of one of our company's smaller plantations, became the acting manager for six months. While in the U.K., Toms resigned, whereupon Edge was made the new permanent manager. This led to a clash in furlough plans. Both Edge and I were scheduled for furlough the following year. To maintain some managerial continuity while Edge was on furlough, I agreed to have my furlough advanced to the 1949/1950 winter. This change had a significant impact on my personal life.

After four-and-a-half months in England, visiting my parents and my two married sisters, it was time to return to India. I said Goodbye to my father at the London Victoria railway station. Walking to the train that would take me to Southampton, I looked back and give a final wave to my dear old dad. I had a premonition I wouldn't see him again, but I dismissed the thought as I got into the train.

Aboard the SS *Canton,* a large Pacific and Orient (P&O) liner, I stood by the railing, watching the tugboats nudge her away from the quayside. She slowly made her way out of the harbor and into the English Channel. The journey began with a violent storm in the Bay of Biscay. The ship rolled and pitched so much that furniture in the large lounge broke loose. It was quite an experience to sit in an easy chair and have it slide from one side of the lounge to the other with each roll. All but a handful of the passengers, and many of the crew, were confined to their cabins with seasickness.

Throughout the first two days the *Canton* was like a ghost ship. I never saw more than nine or ten passengers in the dining room. It was the worst storm I ever experienced in my seven ocean voyages. Fortunately I have never suffered from either seasickness or airsickness.

On the third day out, after we passed through the Strait of Gibraltar into the Mediterranean Sea, the ship quickly came alive as the passengers undid the straps which had prevented them from being thrown from their bunks, and crawled out of their cabins. Their misery was over. Some said they had wanted to die! By the afternoon, though it was still March, we were enjoying glorious Mediterranean sunshine.

The next day the ship was sailing through a becalmed sea. With no wind, there was only a gentle swell, and the surface was like glass. Wanting a little exercise, I took a walk around the promenade deck. After a few turns around the deck, I saw a very attractive Chinese girl casually leaning against the portside rail. Our eyes met.

When I came around again to that side of the ship, she was still there. Once more our eyes met. I stopped and introduced myself. I learned that she, too, was traveling alone, to rejoin her parents in Hong Kong, which was the final destination of the ship. Her father, who had been a high-ranking official in the Canton Province before it fell to the Communists, was now a successful businessman in Hong Kong.

Her name was Bo Hing Wan, and she was twenty-three years old. She was an intelligent, vivacious young lady. An immediate friendship developed, and we happily enjoyed each other's company for the rest of the journey to Bombay, where I disembarked. It was with regret we said Goodbye, promising to write to each other.

A few weeks after I returned to Dalsingpara, Jack Edge went on furlough, and Fanny Adams, a senior assistant, arrived to be the acting manager. A couple of months later Edge resigned, and Adams was confirmed as the new manager—the third in three years.

Bo Hing and I wrote to each other regularly. About a year later, she wrote to say that she would soon be flying to England and would stop off at Calcutta for a few days so we could meet again. She said she would telegraph the time and date of her arrival at Calcutta. A few days later I was sitting in my office when a telegram was handed to me. Eagerly I tore the envelope open, assuming it would be from Bo Hing. Instead, I read through eyes filling with tears: "Father passed away last night. Letter following." The telegram was from my sister Meriel.

I was stunned. I had to be alone. As I sat in my house, quietly sobbing, the picture of Dad standing on the platform of Victoria Station as we waved to each other came vividly into my mind. In my spiritual emptiness, I was devastated with the bleak thought that I would never see my dad again. This idea continued to prey on my mind.

A couple of weeks later I received Bo Hing's telegram and flew down to Calcutta to meet her. Four days later, when Bo Hing flew on to England, she was wearing a diamond engagement ring. We were engaged to be married. Many letters passed back and forth between us during the coming months.

---

[1] *Mahatma* is a title meaning "Great Soul" and is reserved for only the greatest Indian.

# GOD'S INTERVENTION— GOD'S PROTECTION

While I was in Calcutta, George Forrest, another senior pre-war assistant manager, arrived on the plantation to be the new acting manager while Fanny Adams was on furlough in England. About two months later Adams resigned, and Forrest was confirmed as the new manager—the fourth in four years!

By now I was a heavy smoker, smoking fifty or more cigarettes a day. One morning in the late autumn my house servant awoke me with my customary *pulling ka char* (bedside tea). As was my custom, I reached for a cigarette to enjoy with my cup of tea before getting up. As I drew the first smoke into my mouth, it tasted foul. With a grimace I stubbed out the cigarette. Later that afternoon it dawned on me that I had gone all day without smoking; the urge to do so was gone.

I had often tried to give up smoking but without success. As Mark Twain said, "Giving up smoking is easy. I've done it a thousand times." But now, with no conscious effort on my part, I was virtually a nonsmoker! I wondered how long this would last. (It has lasted fifty-three years. I now understand that while I slept God had again intervened in my godless life and had cleansed all nicotine from my body.) Shrugging my shoulders, I went on with my boozing, blasphemous way of life.

But God was still patient, biding His time before again intervening in my life. A few weeks later, one Saturday evening, He did so again.

It was our weekly club day. After a vigorous afternoon of tennis and a tasty English tea catered by the ladies, we drifted into the clubhouse for a shower. After a few games of snooker, three or four other bachelors and I sat around a small table for an evening of whisky drinking. By one o'clock in the morning we were very drunk. The married couples had long before gone home. Somehow the conversation turned to alcoholism. Hayward, one of the mangers, was drinking by himself at home, while his wife was in England, putting their son into a boarding school. We decided Hayward must be an alcoholic.

One of our group then said, "It's all very well calling Hayward an alcoholic. We're all alcoholics."

This brought forth loud protests from the rest of us. "What do you mean, we're alcoholics?" another man demanded.

"We wouldn't be drinking like this if we weren't alcoholics," the first man asserted.

Within my besotted brain God implanted a seed of rebellion against such an idea. Squinting at the glass of whisky I was holding unsteadily in my hand, I slurred, "You mean I'm under the control of this stuff?"

"Sure, you're under its control."

Continuing to squint at my glass, trying to bring it into focus, I hiccupped, "You mean I *have* to drink this stuff?"

"Sure, you have to drink it."

With a blasphemous oath, I banged my glass down on the table and pushed it away. "I won't touch the stuff again," I declared with drunken bravado!

"Oh, shut up, Curnow," they chorused. And downing their drinks, the party broke up.

The next morning, instead of waking up late with a thick head, remembering little about the previous night, I awoke early, with my mind as clear as a bell. The dominating thought in my mind was, *I am not an alcoholic, and I won't drink alcohol again.* I believe that God cleansed my system of all traces of alcohol while I slept that night, just as He had done with nicotine. At the same time He removed all desire for alcohol.

Meanwhile, Bo Hing and I were continuing our plans. I sent her money so she could fly to Calcutta. (This was years before the Boeing 707 transformed international travel, making ocean liners obsolete.) I usually spent Sunday evenings reading, with western pop music playing softly in the background from Radio Ceylon, a shortwave radio station located in Sri Lanka. However, at 9 P.M. the music would be interrupted for half an hour by a religious program which did not interest me, and I would turn off the radio.

One Sunday evening, shortly after I had become a teetotaler, something very strange happened. When the religious program began and I reached to turn off the radio, my hand stopped, immobile, halfway to the knob. I could not move my arm. I was now a captive audience, forced to listen to a male quartet singing, "Lift up the trumpet, and loud let it ring; Jesus is coming again." The radio program was the *Voice of Prophecy*.

This unnerving experience left me stripped of all arrogant ridicule and rejection. *"Jesus is coming again."* Puzzled, in a disturbed frame of mind, I wondered what the words meant. For the first time since those lonely days of solitary confinement in Germany, God had again gotten my attention. The unseen Being released my hand and it fell to my side. I had a compelling feeling that I must continue to listen. The speaker's quiet, informal reasoning and logic gripped me in a way I couldn't explain. I knew I had to listen to him again.

The following week, when the *Voice of Prophecy* program began, I put down my book and listened attentively. After some announcements, the King's Heralds quartet began singing, "There is a place of quiet rest, near to the heart of God." I found my heart being strangely stirred. Then, while the quartet hummed in the background, the speaker, H. M. S. Richards, Sr., began quoting the chorus:

"O Jesus, blest Redeemer,
Sent from the heart of God,
Hold us, who wait before Thee,
Near to the heart of God."

His voice sounded to me like one from heaven itself, and the Holy Spirit came upon me with overpowering conviction.

Suddenly the sinfulness of my life filled me with overwhelming remorse, and I fell to my knees beside the radio, hot tears streaming down my cheeks. In deep, profound repentance I cried out, "O God, forgive me." And just as suddenly as my heart had been convicted of sin, so now, in a moment of time, a wondrous peace flooded my soul. I knew I was forgiven.

I arose from my knees a new creature. The things I had scoffed at and ridiculed were now the desires of my heart, and the sinful things that had been so pleasurable and desirable were now abhorrent to my soul. On my knees beside that radio, I had experienced the miracle of God's amazing grace.

Shortly after becoming a Christian I responded to the *Voice of Prophecy's* invitation to enroll in a Bible study course. I asked for a Bible since I didn't have one.

In my letters to Bo Hing I started telling her about my love for Jesus. I wanted so much for her to become a Christian too. But after a while I could tell she was becoming antagonistic to my conversion. I wrote to the *Voice of Prophecy* about this. The response I received directed my attention to 2 Corinthians 6:14 where God's Word told me, "Do not be unequally yoked together with unbelievers" (NKJV). I knew then that I would have to choose between Jesus, my Savior, and Bo Hing.

One day I received a letter in which she wrote, "Stop writing about this man Jesus; I'm not interested in him." I sadly wrote back, "I cannot stop writing about Jesus . . . I don't think I will hear from you again." I never received another letter from her.

I continued to study the Bible and learn more about the great sacrifice of Christ on the cross. As my love for Him grew, I desired more and more to know and to do His will for my life. To take my mind away from Bo Hing, I became more engrossed with my work on the tea plantation. At the same time, I could not bring myself to throw away her photographs.

George Forrest, the new manager, was scheduled to have a six-month furlough that summer. Due to the spate of resignations by both managers and pre-war senior assistant managers, the company appointed me as acting manager, even though I had only six years of service. This was a pleasant surprise as such appointments had, up to then, been made only after about fifteen years of service.

Later in the summer Forrest also resigned—the fourth manager to resign in four years. The company was now facing a management crisis. I was due my next furlough the following year, but because I knew the predicament the company was in, I offered to postpone my furlough for a year to help relieve the situation. The company responded by appointing me as the new permanent manager of Dalsingpara—the fifth in five years.

However, this annual change of management had led to unstable labor relations, and by the time I took charge, the Revolutionary Socialist Party (RSP), a militant, left-wing trade union, had gained a foothold on the plantation. Increasingly the RSP was intimidating the labor force, resulting in growing tensions between it and the moderate, long-established, Congress Party trade union. I carefully watched this interunion strife, wondering how and when it would affect my management.

Tensions continued to simmer throughout the autumn and winter months when only maintenance work was carried out. This was the relaxed, cooler period of the year when we recuperated from the debilitating heat and humidity of the wet monsoon growing season. However, as the leaf-producing season of 1953 began, the RSP union started an all-out effort to wrest power from the long-established Congress union, and virtually take over the management.

The first demand was that I fire Rajman, the head supervisor of the men's labor force and the leader of the Congress trade union. When I refused, the RSP started stirring up labor unrest against management. One morning I was warned that the RSP was going to cause serious trouble at the factory. Knowing the propensity of the organization to violence, I sent a truck to a police station about five miles away. A squad of armed police arrived at the factory compound a few minutes before an angry, unruly mob of about sixty men stormed into the compound on the other side of the factory. They were led by Lal, the local RSP leader.

## GOD'S INTERVENTION—GOD'S PROTECTION

The result of the timely arrival of the police was dramatic. When the shouting hooligans surged around the factory and saw the police with their rifles, the potential riot collapsed like a pricked balloon. The sudden silence was deafening!

The next day I formally found Lal guilty of unruly conduct and issued him a severe warning notice. He took it contemptuously. But I was now beginning to establish a record of his misbehavior. This was necessary in case management needed the future support of the government Labor Department.

Two weeks later, when I was preparing to leave my office for lunch, Lal, with the same group of men, arrived at my office. This time they were quiet and orderly. I went onto the office veranda and asked them what they wanted. A number of them started talking loudly at the same time. I ordered them to be quiet, telling them that Lal was their spokesman and I would listen to him. He swaggered up onto the veranda, again demanding I fire Rajman.

After about an hour of fruitless discussion, I told Lal I was going for lunch. But when I turned to leave, Lal put up his arm to stop me. I saw from the look on his face and the sudden tension of the other men that they intended to forcibly detain me against my will. By this time all the clerical staff and factory workers had quietly gone home. I was alone with Lal and his henchmen.

Slowly the hours passed as the standoff continued, with their tempers flaring from time to time and then subsiding. It was a test of wills, and I knew violence was one of their weapons. My weapon was prayer, which I was using all the time. The prayer I quietly offered up to God many times during those hours was *O God, overrule this evil.*

After some six hours, at about 6 P.M., when the mood of the mob was deteriorating, I heard a car drive up and stop on the other side of the office building. A moment later John Tibbett, the acting manager of Toorsa Tea Estate, walked through the office to the veranda. He immediately summed up the situation. Realizing it was imperative that the men understood everything that was said if he was to be allowed to leave, he asked in Hindustani, *"Kia horta hai?"* ("What's going on?")

*"Kuch ne. Kalli bhatchit korta ha"* ("Nothing. Just talking."), I replied. And then, without moving my lips, I said softly, "Get the police."

With a shrug of his shoulders he said, *"Tik hai. Hum tumko pitchee dekega."* ("OK. I'll see you later.") As he turned to leave, he whispered, "Got the message." And with that he was allowed to drive away.

With relief I expected him to return with the police well within the hour. But as one hour dragged into two, time and Lal's patience were running out. He would stand in front of me, with his face only inches from mine, and scream at me. His eyes took on a glazed look, and he frothed at the mouth; his jugular veins stood out like cords. He had only to strike me and the mob would have gone berserk.

"O God. Control his madness," I whispered.

After a few minutes he would calm down, but his explosive outbursts of rage became more frequent.

*John, where are you?* I kept asking myself in desperation. I believed that now, after eight hours, time had run out. If I was to avoid injury or worse I would have to give in, surrendering my managerial authority to a thug.

Suddenly there was a shout, *"Police ai gia"* ("Police have come."), and the men started running around to the other side of the building. As I turned to go through the office, I whispered a prayer of thanks to God.

Entering the assistant's office I saw Tibbett, a police sergeant, and two constables. Tibbett said, "Sorry I took so long. I'll explain later." At the back of the building the mob started up the steps of the veranda, but the two constables crossed their rifles in front of the door to prevent the men from getting into the office.

While the sergeant was trying to calm them, I saw one of the men, a Nepalese worker, begin to pull his kukri[1] from its scabbard. Pointing to the man I said, *"Sergeant. Dekko!"* ("Sergeant. Look!") The man quickly pushed the *kukri* back into the scabbard as the sergeant warned him of dire consequences if he unsheathed it again. That incident sent cold shivers down my spine. *Why was that man carrying such a lethal weapon?*

Having lost the initiative, the dissidents quickly lost steam and dispersed. Tibbett then explained he had thought to save time by getting the Border Patrol police stationed on his plantation, it being next to Bhutan. However, they were out on patrol, and he had to look for them. I told him he had arrived just in time and that it couldn't have been closer.

The next day I charged Lal with gross insubordination and assault against the manager. Finding him guilty, I issued him with another severe warning notice.

For two or three weeks the RSP laid low, but one day I was informed there was going to be major trouble at the afternoon leaf weighing. As the first pickers arrived, instead of weighing their leaf and going home, they waited silently. Following the advice of the supervisors, David Waters, my young assistant manager, and I stood about thirty feet away.

It wasn't long before all one thousand workers were gathered, waiting quietly. The RSP had threatened them with physical assault if they weighed their leaf. I told Waters that if the dissidents made any move toward us, we should go to the office where we could have our backs to a wall and not be surrounded.

After about fifteen minutes the troublemakers started shouting and moving toward us. I told Waters, "Let's go." But as we started to walk away about sixty men began running. I said, "Dave. Stop. We must face them."

When we turned around, they halted about twenty-five feet away and fell silent. I stood with my legs apart, my hands on my hips, leaning slightly forward. I looked unwaveringly at Lal until he lowered his eyes. I did the same with the other leaders.

All the while I was praying, *Lord, I don't owe these workers anything. I am being a Christian manager. Overrule this evil. And please don't let fear show on my face.*

Then, misjudging the situation, I said to Waters, "Let's go." But as soon as we turned, the mob again started shouting and running toward us.

"Stop, David," I said urgently as I whipped round to face them once again.

The mob again stopped and fell silent, this time about fifteen feet away. Again I stared Lal and the others down, all the time praying that God would overrule. Whenever they looked at me I stared at them until, one by one, they started turning sideways and looking at me over their shoulders. Finally I said to Waters, "We can go now, David." And with that we walked away in silence.

Before we reached the office we heard the baskets of leaves being weighed. It was a total moral victory. The RSP hooligans had been completely discredited in front of the whole labor force, including the factory workers who had been watching through the factory windows. It wasn't two lone Englishmen who had successfully faced down sixty thugs. I believe they sensed they were facing a supernatural power they could neither understand nor resist. The unseen presence of a mighty angel of God can be the only rational answer to that amazing outcome.

The trade union collapsed, its influence totally evaporated. The outside leaders withdrew from the plantation, and I fired Lal. Because of the record against him, the government Labor Department upheld his dismissal, rejecting his claim I was victimizing him because he was a union leader. From then on I had harmonious labor relationships. The workers knew I would stand firm in looking after the company's interests, but they also knew they had a manager who would look after their interests as well.

---

[1] A Nepalese hunting and fighting weapon with a heavy fourteen-inch curved blade. In World War II it was used with devastating effect against the Japanese by the famed Nepalese Ghurka soldiers.

# A GOD-DIRECTED ROMANCE

I continued studying the Bible lessons from the *Voice of Prophecy* and listening each Sunday to the messages of H. M. S. Richards, Sr. One Sunday he had a question-and-answer program. One of the questions was "What denomination sponsors the *Voice of Prophecy?*" Richards answered, "I am an ordained minister of the Seventh-day Adventist Church." Shortly after that I studied a lesson dealing with God's true Sabbath. As I studied this topic in the Bible I was surprised to learn the biblical Sabbath was Saturday, the seventh day of the week, and that Sunday observance was a tradition stemming from the early papal church. After becoming a Christian I had started keeping Sunday in a worshipful manner. I now changed to keeping the Sabbath. Since I was no longer working on Saturday, which was a workday on the plantation, I went to my office on Sunday when I could work quietly with nothing to disturb me. This did not fully satisfy my superiors, however.

The following year, while on furlough, I attended a Board meeting of the Nedeem Tea Company in London, seeking a solution to the fact that I was not working on Saturday. At that time, there was general labor unrest on the tea plantations, and Mr. Nicholls, the chairman, said, "Curnow, we have one question to ask you. What would you do if there were a riot on Saturday?"

I replied, "I would consider it my duty as a Christian to use both my personal influence and that of the manager to prevent any harm to either persons or property."

*With H. M. S. Richards, Sr., at the* Voice of
Prophecy *headquarters in Glendale, California,
1970—sixteen years after my baptism*

"That's all we wanted to hear, Curnow. Carry on as you are doing. And have a good furlough."

Later in the year I learned that Elder Richards would be on a world tour and would be the guest speaker at a *Voice of Prophecy* rally in Calcutta. I timed my annual vacation so I could attend. It was a thrilling and inspirational experience to meet the tall, slender man with thick-lensed spectacles, whose soft-spoken, persuasive voice had captured my heart for Jesus Christ. Besides meeting Elder Richards, I also met Elder A. E. Rawson, the *Voice of Prophecy* director in India. I planned with him to complete the advanced Bible course by the following April, by which time I would be returning to England on my next furlough. Rawson suggested I be baptized at the Southern Asia Division headquarters of the Seventh-day Adventist Church located at Poona (Pune) before I left India. This would be ideal since Poona was near to Bombay (Mombai), where I would be boarding ship.

Elder Rawson told me about Raymond Memorial School, a Seventh-day Adventist mission school near Falakata, only twenty-five miles south of Dalsingpara. When I visited the school I received a warm, open-hearted welcome by the principal, Lenny Hare, and his wife Esther. I had never experienced such friendliness before. I felt like part of their family. They invited me to spend every Sabbath with them, and so began a tradition that lasted until they returned to America. Our friendship has continued now for more than fifty years.

# A GOD-DIRECTED ROMANCE

In early April 1954, I handed over the management of Dalsing-para to Max Warner, the new manager (I would be returning to manage the Nya Sylee Tea Estate, about seventy miles to the west), and excitedly prepared to leave on furlough. The previous Sabbath, Lenny and Esther Hare had urged me, "Now John, be sure to come back with a lovely Christian wife. We'll be praying for you."

A week later Elder Rawson baptized me in the Poona church. Coming up out of the water and seeing the smiling face of Elder Rawson was an experience never to fade from my memory. I knew that I was now a part of God's family. The stark contrast between the life I was now living and the old way was well illustrated by the words of John Newton's immortal hymn "Amazing Grace": "I once was lost but now am found, was blind but now I see."

When Elder Rawson and his wife Elsie drove me to Bombay to catch my ship, they also urged me to find a Christian wife. Elder Rawson gave me a letter of introduction to Elder C. R. Bonney, his counterpart in England, so that the church there would know who I was.

One sunny afternoon, as the ship was steaming westward through the Mediterranean toward the Strait of Gibraltar and the Atlantic Ocean, I was leaning against the ship's railing, gazing at the sea which stretched like a vast mirror to the horizon. My mind went back four years to a similar day when I had met Bo Hing Wan on the SS *Canton*. I went to my cabin and took out her photographs which I still had. Opening the porthole, I looked at them for the last time and threw them out into the sea. I found myself biting my lip as I watched them disappear from my view.

I knelt in prayer. "O Lord, You told me, 'Do not be unequally yoked with an unbeliever,' and I have obeyed You. But may I remind You of something else You have said in the Bible, 'It is not good for man to be alone.' You know I will soon be thirty-one and returning to India for another three years. I don't want to remain a bachelor. I believe you have my life's partner waiting for me in England. I leave it entirely in Your hands."

Three days later the liner hove to in Tor Bay, Devon, to take aboard customs and immigration officials before continuing along the English Channel to Tilbury Dock in London. The brilliance of the varied patchwork of green fields covering the rolling Devon hills made many foreign passengers gasp in amazement as they crowded the railings.

It was wonderful to arrive home and see my mother again. I greatly missed my dad. For the first time he wasn't there to welcome me home. I regretted he had not lived to see me become a Christian.

A few days later I took a fifteen-mile bus ride to Stanborough Park, Watford, where the headquarters of the Seventh-day Adventist Church in England was located. Finding Elder Bonney, I handed him the letter of introduction from Elder Rawson. He greeted me warmly, being especially interested to learn I had become a Christian through the *Voice of Prophecy.*

When I asked Elder Bonney about a nearby church, he suggested, "Why don't you come to the church here at Stanborough Park? It is only fifteen miles from where you are staying." With a twinkle in his eye he added, "This is a large church, and there are a lot of young people here." (In his letter of introduction, Elder Rawson had asked Elder Bonney to help me find a wife.)

After the service that first Sabbath hundreds of members gathered in small groups outside church, chatting and laughing. I suddenly felt very lonely in the midst of the crowd. After a minute or so a young man approached me. Extending his hand, he said, "I believe you are a visitor. I'm Mervyn Whiting."

I told him I had just arrived on furlough from India where I had been recently baptized. Learning I did not live in the Watford area, he invited me home for lunch, where I met his wife, Iris. They were a warm, friendly young couple in their early twenties, being newlyweds of just two or three months. After lunch we spent a pleasant afternoon together.

The next Sabbath Mervyn took me to the smaller Watford Town Church for the afternoon Young Peoples meeting. In the evening, an hour before sundown, we attended a similar youth meeting at the Stanborough Park Church.

After the meeting, Mervyn said, "Let me introduce you to some of the young people." I felt happy about that! There were maybe fifty or more young people gathered in groups outside the church, but as we walked through them, he ignored them, except to return a greeting. He was looking for a particular person. Finally he saw her with her parents.

"Joan," he called.

The young lady walked toward us.

"Joan, I want you to meet a new friend of mine, John Curnow. He has just come home from India on furlough. John, this is Joan Gallaher."

I noticed she became slightly flustered. She told me later that when I stepped forward to shake her hand, Mervyn had given her a meaningful wink over my shoulder as if to say, "I've found him for you. He's your man!" Joan was the only one of his circle of friends who was not married.

Before we could chat, her father called out, "Joan. It's time for us to go." With a hasty, "Nice to have met you," she hurried back to her parents.

Mervyn did not introduce me to any other young lady.

After Joan had left, I learned from him that though Joan was only twenty-three, she was already a registered nurse, a certified midwife, and was currently taking a health visitor's course at a college in London. Mervyn also told me that her father was the physiotherapist and radiologist at the Stanborough Hydro, the Seventh-day Adventist sanitarium at Stanborough Park, and was also a deacon and organist at the church. Her mother was a semi-retired nurse at the Hydro. Her only uncle worked at the Stanborough Publishing House at the Park, and her two aunts had worked for the church. I was impressed by her family background.

The next Sabbath I met Joan after church, and we chatted for about fifteen minutes. During the week I began praying about this young lady to whom I had been introduced. Was she the one God had waiting for me?

The next Sabbath I again met Joan outside the church. During the church service it was announced that two seats were still available on the chartered bus taking church members to the graduation at Newbold College the following day.

Joan asked if I would like to go. When I said Yes she went back into the church. A few minutes later she returned. "I was able to book the last seat for you." Did I detect a little excitement in her voice as she said that? Since the bus would pass about two miles from my mother's house, I arranged to meet the bus where two highways joined.

The next morning when I climbed aboard the bus, I was conscious that fifty pairs of eyes were scrutinizing me intently. After all, Joan Gallaher was a well regarded Stanborough Park girl, and who was this "stranger from India"? I sat down in the vacant seat beside her.

While at the graduation Joan told me that, because of the Whitsun holiday, the next weekend would be a long one and that the Young Peoples Society of the Stanborough Church was planning a campout at Wallingford, a beauty spot on the River Thames. She was going with several of her friends and asked whether I would care to join the group. Having been a keen camper when younger, I agreed to go.

She told me I wouldn't need to worry about a tent because there would be two large ones, one for the men and another for the ladies. There would also be several smaller tents for the chaperoning families.

During the week I earnestly prayed, asking God to make it clear whether Joan was the one He had chosen to be my life's partner. At the same time I was not letting myself become emotionally involved. As I observed Joan during the three days of the campout, and saw her interaction with her many friends, it was very apparent she was a fine, intelligent, and gracious young Christian lady. But I still kept a tight lid on my emotions. What would be her feelings toward me in the short time I would be in England?

While we sat beside each other in the chartered bus on the way back to Stanborough Park, God gave me the conviction that Joan was the one He had kept waiting for me. For the first time I took her hand, and as she looked at me I was sure I saw love in her eyes.

I escorted her home, and she invited me in. All was quiet, for her parents and young brother were on vacation. Slowly I walked up to her and placed my hands on her shoulders.

"Joan, I have a question I want to ask you."

"Yes?" she replied softly.

"Joan. Will you marry me and come with me to India?"

Without any hesitation she replied, "I'd love to."

When I heard those words, I gazed in wonderment at this lovely young lady, who was eight years younger than I. She really didn't know me, and yet she was still willing to make this life-changing commitment. I fell deeply in love with her. Just twenty-three days after being introduced to each other we were engaged.

I arranged to be with Joan when her parents arrived back from their vacation the following Friday. Seeing the car arrive, we went out to meet them. Joan introduced me to her parents only as John. She couldn't remember my last name, which she had heard only once or twice. While I helped my future father-in-law unpack the car, Mrs. Gallaher hurried inside to put the kettle on to boil, followed by Joan.

As her mother bustled around the kitchen, Joan nervously asked, "Mummy, what do you think of him?"

"Who?"

"John. You just met him out at the car."

" Oh. A nice young man."

"Yes, Mummy, but he has asked me to marry him."

"How wonderful, my dear."

"But, Mummy, he's going to take me to India."

"Oh, how exciting," was all my marvelous future mother-in-law had to say.

Ten weeks later Joan and I were married, and Mervyn Whiting, who had become nervous because of the speed at which our engagement and marriage was taking place, was my best man. Elder C. R. Bonney performed the marriage.

*Joan and I on our wedding day only five months after my baptism*

# FOLLOWING ABRAHAM'S EXAMPLE

Three weeks after our wedding, the Polish liner *Batori,* on which we were traveling, steamed out of Southampton. After brief stops at Gibraltar, Port Said, Aden, and Karachi, we arrived at Bombay, where Elder Rawson met us. We spent a few delightful days with the Rawsons before traveling on to Calcutta and then to our final destination, Nya Sylee Tea Estate.

I faced a daunting challenge as I took over the management of this plantation. It had incurred losses for the past fourteen years, and the company had tried, unsuccessfully, to sell it. Would I be able to turn things around? I was optimistic as I saw that the plantation had excellent potential. The basic problem had been long-term mismanagement, leading to debilitating apathy on the part of the field labor force and low standards of production in the factory. It was gratifying to see how quickly the workers responded to a management guided fully by Christian principles and ethics. The following year, 1955, was an exciting and memorable one. Nya Sylee made its first profit in fifteen years, but more importantly, 1955 saw the birth of our daughter, Sally Anne.

A few weeks before Sally was born, we sent our six-month-old leopard to the Dudley Zoo in England. It had been brought to us when it was only a few days old. Hunters had found it, with two other cubs, in a nearby jungle. We purchased two of the cubs, which Joan named Bo Bo and Bingo. Unfortunately, while they were still very small, our Labrador dog killed Bingo. My house servant rescued Bo Bo just in time.

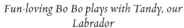

*Fun-loving Bo Bo plays with Tandy, our Labrador*

*Bo Bo (five months) sunbathing after a swim in his favorite creek*

Bo Bo behaved like a dog. It slept on the foot of our bed, and when we sat on the sofa, it would lie along the back, acting as a cushion for our heads. It liked to swing on the curtains and would lie for an hour at a time looking through the wire mesh at our chickens. As it grew larger, Tandy, our dog, treated it warily. We were sorry to see it go, but didn't fancy the thought of a rapidly growing leopard, however tame, snuggling up in the baby's crib.

After a year and a half at Nya Sylee I was asked to take over the management of Chengmari, the company's largest estate. With 6,665 acres, it was the second-largest tea plantation in India. Its workforce of just over 3,200 lived on the estate, along with about 3,500 dependants.

Though life on the plantation was absorbing and rich with so many varied experiences, the highpoint of each week was our visit on Sabbath to Raymond Memorial School, at Falakata. Lenny and Esther Hare had been thrilled to meet Joan and had immediately embraced her with love and friendship.

But all was not tranquil within my heart. Shortly after becoming a Christian I had been sitting in my office when Max Warner, the manager of Toorsa, walked in. Without responding to my greeting, he asked, "These people you are studying the Bible with, did you say they are Seventh-day Adventists?"

"Yes. Why do you ask?"

"Did you know they don't drink tea?"

"What! Where did you hear that?" I asked in surprise.

"I read it in my encyclopedia."

For a moment I had sat in stunned silence. "I can't believe it," I had said. "What on earth has tea got to do with religion?"

"Come to my place and you can read it for yourself," Warner had replied.

Getting into our cars, I had followed Warner back to Toorsa.

There it was in the encyclopedia, "Seventh-day Adventists don't smoke tobacco or opium, nor drink tea, coffee, or alcohol."

I had sat in disbelief that tea would be linked with tobacco, alcohol, and opium. After all, surely offering a person a cup of tea was like offering him a glass of orange juice.

That evening I had written to the *Voice of Prophecy* about it. They had replied that, for health reasons, the church advocated abstinence from tea and coffee, but that such abstinence was not a requirement for church membership. Not being convinced that tea was unhealthful, I had dismissed the matter from my mind.

But through the three years since first meeting the Hares, they and other Adventist missionaries had quietly, but steadfastly, abstained from tea, and this disturbed me. I now began wondering whether I should remain in the tea industry. *But this is my life,* I would tell myself as I pushed the matter from my mind.

One Sabbath in the summer of 1956, Lenny Hare preached a sermon about the rich young ruler who had come to meet Jesus. That evening, as we drove the sixty miles back to Chengmari, I was quiet. Finally Joan asked me, "John, is anything the matter?"

"The sermon Lenny preached this morning. I can't stop thinking that I may be that rich young ruler who turned sorrowfully away from Jesus. Compared with the missionaries, I'm pretty rich. At thirty-three I'm young, and, being a plantation manager, with thousands of workers under me, I'm certainly a 'ruler.' Is Jesus telling me to 'sell' everything and follow Him? I don't know."

With troubled heart and mind, I continued driving in silence.

We had just finished lunch one day a few weeks later, when I received a copy of *The Visitor,* the monthly church magazine of the Northeast India Union of Seventh-day Adventists. Joan went into the living room while I stayed at the table looking through *The Visitor.* The theme of the lead article by William F. Storz, the union president, was temperance. After touching briefly on its basic principles, he turned to the subject of tea in a candid and straight forward manner.

My initial reaction was to dismiss what I was reading as irrelevant, just as I had been doing for the past three years whenever confronted with the subject. But then Elder Storz began quoting extensively from the writings of Ellen White. I was fully persuaded that Ellen White had fulfilled the Bible promise of the gift of prophecy to the church prior to Christ's return. So I was stunned when I read the many quotations in the article, three of which were "Tea is poisonous to the system" (*Counsels on Diet and Food,* p. 421). "Tea and coffee drinking is a sin" (Ibid., p. 425). "The only safe course is to touch not, taste not, handle not, tea, coffee, wines, tobacco, opium, and alcoholic drinks" (Ibid., p. 428). And I was growing and manufacturing tea!

This Spirit of Prophecy counsel was unequivocal. Elder Storz had pulled the rug from under me.

With my mind spinning, I looked for Joan. When I walked into the living room, she looked up from where she was kneeling by the fireplace, tidying some papers.

"John! What is wrong?" (She told me later that I looked awful!)

"Joan, listen to this," and I read some of the quotations.

"I never knew Mrs. White had said anything like that," Joan said with perplexity. "What shall we do?"

"Ellen White claimed she received her counsels to the church from God while in vision. There are only three alternatives. She was either a blasphemous charlatan, taking the name of the Lord in vain. Or she was a deluded fool, not knowing what she was talking about. Or she was in truth God's special servant to whom He had given these counsels. If we believe either of the first two alternatives, we will soon leave the church. It has to be the third.

This is God speaking directly to us through His servant."

I knew what I had to do, and taking Joan's hands in mine, I said, "Joan, we have to leave tea." Nodding her head, she replied, "Yes, John, you're right."

We knelt in prayer, asking God to lead us into the unknown future. I felt a burden had been lifted from me. I was no longer resisting the still, small voice of the Holy Spirit.

We stopped drinking tea, and shortly afterward we became vegetarians. I informed the company that I would not be asking for my contract to be renewed when it expired at the end of the following year.

The year 1956 ended with great joy when our son Adrian was born on December 29.

# IN PARTNERSHIP WITH GOD ON THREE CONTINENTS

Because Jim Robinson, the new manager, was taking a winter furlough, the company asked me to stay on until he returned in the early spring of 1958.

Shortly before we left Chengmari a tragedy occurred. A man-eating tiger moved into the jungle area on the southern end of the plantation. It killed and partially ate one of our factory workers who had gone into the jungle to gather firewood. Thereafter, until we left Chengmari, we did not allow our two small children outside of the house. Sally couldn't understand why she could no longer go outside to smell the flowers. It was a tense time for everyone in the district, and a major effort was made to hunt the animal down and shoot it. Before we left India we heard that it had been killed.

When we arrived back in England, Joan's parents and my mother were thrilled to see their grandchildren for the first time.

As I looked to the future I had a strong desire to become a minister. I visited Elder McMillan, president of the British Union Conference, to ask his advice. He pointed out that I would be forty years old by the time I had completed the four-year ministerial course at Newbold College. He suggested I become a literature evangelist. Elder Rawson had also suggested this before we left India.

Following this advice, I entered the literature evangelistic work and began selling a beautiful set of books, *Footprints of Jesus,* by W. L. Emmerson, editor of the Stanborough Press. The books, which covered the life and ministry of Christ, were highly illustrated with scores of reproductions of old masterpieces. This gave me the opportunity to pray in many homes. A lady in the village of Great Offley in Bedforshire told me that as a result of my praying in over eighty homes in the village, the local Methodist Church board had decided to start having midweek prayer meetings for the first time in over thirty years.

One day while driving along a country road, I saw a gypsy horse-drawn caravan parked in a meadow. One of the gypsies was excited when he saw the books. "I want these books. I can't read myself, but my daughter is going to school, and she will be able to read them to me. Anyway, these pictures tell the story of Jesus."

Continuing along the country road I came to a private drive. Turning through the open gateway with its large wrought-iron gates, I saw the roofline of one of the grand stately homes of England above a row of tall ornamental trees. I stopped at a cottage nearby and inquired who lived in the great house. "It's the estate of Lord David Bowes-Lyon, the brother of the Queen Mother and uncle of Queen Elizabeth," I was told.

I pulled the bell-chain and heard a sound echo through the cavernous hallway, a hallway so large that my house could easily have fit into it twice over!

Lady Bowes-Lyon, herself, answered the door and graciously invited me in. She readily purchased the books and warmly thanked me for the prayer I offered before I left. Providentially, it was the butler's day off, for certainly he would have turned me away! That morning I saw what a wonderful ministry the colporteur work is and how it could touch the lives of everyone, from the lowly gypsy to the highborn auntie of the Queen of England.

After two years, during which time Ian, our second son, was born, I was invited to join the South England Publishing Department as associate director. Eighteen months later I was appointed as the director.

Two years later, in the spring of 1964, we answered a call from the Southern Asia Division to return to India to be publishing director for the South India Union. Once again Joan and I were on the high seas, this time with four young children. Perryn, our third son, had joined the family through adoption. Joan and I were thrilled to be back in India, a country we loved dearly. This time we were located in south India, which is so different from north India, yet in many ways the same. After three years in India, I was ordained into the ministry. Shortly afterward, Johannes Johanson, the union president, asked me to be the principal of Lowery Memorial Higher Secondary School.

"Johannes, you know my educational background," I replied in complete surprise.

"Yes, but you have successfully managed a tea plantation with three thousand workers, and I believe you can manage a boarding school with five hundred and fifty children."

"That's a new twist," I replied with a grin. I agreed to take on the challenge.

The two years we were at Lowry were both challenging and rewarding, as I was able to improve the fiscal strength of the school, while Monickam Dhason, the head master, raised the school's academic level.

In 1969, I was appointed Publishing Department director for the Southern Asia Division, located in Poona. Joan became one of the two teachers of the small church school for the children of the numerous missionary families connected with the division headquarters and Spicer College, located about eight miles away. My appointment as publishing director led to extensive travel throughout India and the other countries within the division territory. Travel, whether by bus, train, or plane, gave me many opportunities to introduce fellow travelers to the *Voice of Prophecy* Bible correspondence courses.

On one flight from Bombay to Calcutta, I had handed out enrollment cards, with a short explanatory letter, to each of the passengers. Just before landing I collected the cards and received thirty-seven requests for Bible and health courses—and the flight attendant did not even tell me to sit down and buckle up! On another flight, the flight attendant told me the captain wanted to know what I was doing. I gave her some cards to show him. She returned with the cards filled out by the captain. On an extended trip by bus and train,

I brought back 122 completed enrollment cards. It gave me great joy to introduce fellow travelers to the Lord Jesus who was waiting to lead them along the pathway to heaven.

In 1975 we were returning to India after a furlough. I left Joan and Perryn, our youngest son, at London's Heathrow airport to handle our luggage and boarding passes, while Ian, our middle son, and I returned our car to a dealer in London. While she waited for us to return, Joan chatted with an English girl, Mandy, who was on our flight. Finally, the other passengers began boarding the plane, and still I had not appeared. Joan became more and more anxious. Meanwhile, I was urging the taxi driver to hurry!

We were booked on Egypt Air, a discount airline which did not have assigned seating and whose Boeing 707 was fully booked. At last Ian and I made it to the airport and hurried to the gate. The four of us were the last to board the plane, and we looked for the four unoccupied seats, hoping the airline hadn't overbooked! Finding seats for Ian and Perryn, Joan and I moved down the aisle to the rear of the plane where we found the last two unoccupied seats—next to the young lady Joan had been chatting with earlier!

As we flew south to Cairo, Mandy Barrett told us of her very unhappy childhood, broken engagement, and nervous breakdown. She was traveling to India to work with a Hindu organization engaged in village welfare. She was hoping to find some meaningful purpose for her life.

After an overnight stop in Cairo we continued our journey to Bombay. Mandy told us she had been booked on a flight the previous week, but had cancelled due to sickness. Egypt Air was always fully booked weeks in advance, so normally she would have had to wait several weeks for another flight. But, surely providentially, she was given a seat on our flight, and we were sitting beside her!

Since there hadn't been enough time to notify the Hindu organization of her changed schedule (this was before the days of instant satellite communications), I asked Mandy what she planned to do when she arrived in Bombay.

"Oh, I'll stay in a hotel until I can contact the organization and get instructions," she replied.

"Mandy," I responded, "there are some excellent five-star hotels in Bombay, but they would clean out your limited funds in a few days. Regarding the other types of hotels, I would not let my daughter stay alone in one. Why don't you stay with us in Poona until you hear from your people? Our daughter is in college in America, so you could have her room."

After a little hesitation, she agreed. I think she was a little nervous about getting too close to missionaries, especially Seventh-day Adventists.

When the church bell started ringing the first Wednesday evening we were home, Mandy asked what it meant.

"That is to remind everyone that the prayer meeting will start in half an hour," I told her.

"What do you do at prayer meeting?"

"We sing some gospel songs, and then there is a short devotional message. After that we separate into small groups for prayer."

"Are you going?"

"Yes, Mandy. Joan and I will be going."

"Can I come, too?"

"Surely," I said with a smile. From then on Mandy never missed a Sabbath or midweek meeting.

On the plane, Mandy had told us that her parents, foster parents, and older brother had all been divorced and that her own engagement had ended violently when her drunken fiancé had hit her on the head with a hammer. "I'm wondering now if I'm in heaven," she said, "because all the married couples here at Salisbury Park are happy. They aren't fighting with each other."

As the days passed, we began to hear her infectious laughter.

After about three weeks, Mandy heard from her Hindu group and left for south India to begin her village work. However, after only a few months she wrote to tell us that she was leaving the group because of pressure to sign false statements regarding the work she was doing. At the same time we had need of a volunteer to look after the Christian Children's Fund (CCF) work at our local mission school. Mandy gladly returned to Salisbury Park to take this job.

One day there was a knock on my office door. When I called "Come in," the door slowly opened, and Mandy peeked around the edge of the door.

"Are you busy, John?" she asked.

"I'm never too busy to have a chat with you, Mandy. What's on your mind?"

"John, you Seventh-day Adventists live such beautiful lives. I want to be one, too. I know you have some teachings that are different, but that doesn't matter. Will you give me Bible studies so I can be baptized?"

Could there be any sweeter "music" to the ear of a pastor? Because of my busy program, I arranged with Eleanor Hetke to give Mandy Bible studies. Everybody loved Mandy, and we had to share her with other missionary families. Eleanor and Elsworth Hetke were one of those families. Not long after this, I had the joy of baptizing Mandy in the same church in which I had been baptized twenty-two years earlier.

The time came for Mandy to return to England. When she arrived home her younger brother, Jonathan, could hardly recognize her; she was not the same girl who had left England a year earlier! "I must meet these Seventh-day Adventist people who have changed my sister like this," he determined. Before the end of the year he, too, was baptized, and the following year he enrolled at Newbold College to study for the ministry. For the past twenty-four years he has been a successful pastor in the South England Conference. The story of Mandy (Barrett) Warren and her brother Jonathan Barrett is another example of God's amazing grace!

During our ten years at Poona, one by one, our children had gone to Far Eastern Academy in Singapore before heading to the United States for college. In 1979 Joan and I decided it was time to follow them to the States so that they would have a home to come to.

When we left India we left behind a part of our hearts in the small cemetery at Salisbury Park. In 1968 we had taken into our home a little two-year-old girl from the Lushai Hills of northeast India. Her mother had died. Very soon Naomi's little fingers had entwined themselves around our hearts. But when she was only four-and-a-half years old this bright, intelligent little girl died suddenly from cerebral meningitis. On her headstone we engraved these words from aching hearts:

God knew our need for sunshine
So He gave her as a loan.
He let us love and keep her,
Till our hearts were bigger grown.

In the United States, I joined the Christian Record Braille Foundation (now Christian Record Services) as a representative in southern California. After six months, on January 1, 1980, I was appointed the area director for CRBF in the Southwestern Union, and, in 1986, I became the national director of Special Projects for CRBF.

Working with, and for, the blind was one of the most satisfying and rewarding ministries in which I have been involved. Being camp coordinator at the National Camps for the Blind in the southwest, though challenging, was very pleasurable. We can learn so much from blind people.

In 1989 I retired from full-time responsibilities, but not from service for the Lord as health, strength, and opportunities permit.

~

My story is one of God's infinite love and amazing grace. His divine "search and rescue mission" intervened in the life of a man hopelessly lost in the dark world of sin. In the words of John Newton, "I once was lost, but now am found; was blind, but now I see." My prayer is that my story may be an encouragement to every reader as he or she awaits the soon return of Jesus Christ.

# EPILOGUE

On August 21, 2003, Joan and I visited Lichfield, Staffordshire, England where my crew had received its final operational training. From there we traveled to Barnetby-le-Wold, Lincolnshire, to attend, for the first time, the annual reunion of my squadron association. Elsham Wolds, the site of the old squadron, was two-and-a-half miles away.

I wanted to be alone with my memories as I again trod, after sixty years, the revered acres of Elsham Wolds. As I was leaving the village, a man working in his front garden greeted me. Learning that I planned to walk the long uphill road to Elsham Wolds, he offered to drive me there. He and a friend took me first to the site of the squadron's main entrance, now a farm gate. The road which led to the squadron offices and airfield was in disrepair. They drove me to the edge of the old airfield, now farmland, and left me alone, since I planned to be there for an hour or so.

As I walked through the stubble of harvested wheat, the quietness was broken only by the wind blowing across the wolds. I paused at one of the eroding runways. In imagination I heard the pulsing engines of the old squadron, which had throbbed with life—and death. During World War II my squadron lost over fifteen hundred airmen killed in action or accidents.

As I slowly wandered in solitude across the farmland, I found myself talking aloud, looking to the sky, and gesticulating as if the "ghosts" of yesteryear could hear. My emotion was intense; a tear trickled down my cheek.

Weeds and grass pushed through a web of cracks in the old main runway. I wondered whether I would recognize the place where we had crashed on takeoff with a full load of bombs and fuel (see chapter 8). I did.

The next morning I was flown over Elsham Wolds in a two-seater plane. The three runways were clearly discernable. Never had I dreamed I would ever again fly over Elsham Wolds and look down

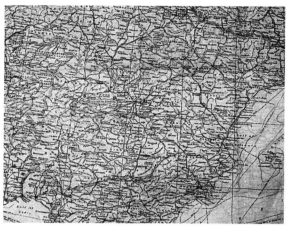

*One of my three silk maps of Europe that I hid from my captors and kept throughout the war*

on the runway from which we had taken off that fateful night so long ago.

At the reunion dinner that evening, I presented one of my silk escape maps to be displayed in the Association's Memorial Room, at which time I gave the following short address:

It was sixty-one years ago, in late August of 1942, when I first arrived at Elsham Wolds as a young nineteen-year-old navigator. So many memories crowd my mind as I think back to those early days on the old Halifax squadron and then later to the new Lancasters; from being the rookie crew to, six months later, being the senior crew and the last of the old Halifax men. And then, on March 10, 1943, the old Halifax squadron was finally gone as we, too, were shot down.

During my six months on the squadron, I saw twenty-seven crews lost with 165 men killed in action, including my own crew, with only twenty-seven survivors, of whom I am one. During that period not one crew had been able to complete a full tour of thirty operations and leave Elsham Wolds alive. These are somber memories as, after sixty years, I have this weekend finally returned to Elsham Wolds.

But ladies and gentlemen, we are gathered here this evening to enjoy excellent food and great company; to renew old friendships and make new ones. And that is how it should be. But I do believe that one of our primary reasons for coming here is to remember and honor those who made the ultimate and supreme sacrifice.

And so, Mr. Chairman, as I present this World War II silk escape map for the Memorial Room, I do so in remembrance of all those young British, Commonwealth, and other airmen who took off from Elsham Wolds, never to return.

This map is one of three I successfully hid from the Germans in the waistband of my trousers and which I used in my four escapes, the first of which was from the French gendarme who initially apprehended me, and the other three from German POW camps. My last escape was successful.

Ladies and gentlemen, may our God-ordained and blood-bought freedom, which we can so easily take for granted, reign for ever!

May God bless each one of you.

The next day a memorial service was conducted on the old squadron site. Wreaths and small crosses were placed at a cenotaph that had been erected there in memory of all the airmen killed from both the 103rd Squadron and the 576th Squadron, which shared Elsham Wolds for the last two years of the war.

At the close of the service, the only serviceable Lancaster bomber in Britain made three low passes over the site. The excitement was electric as the unique roar of its four Merlin engines was first heard and the plane swooped low overhead. Twice it banked around and thundered over our upturned faces. Many eyes were moist as the old bomber finally flew south and disappeared in the distance.

*The unsurpassed Lancaster. In 2003, this is the only serviceable Lancaster still in existence in Britain.*

The next day we took a train for France. At Reims, we were met by Olivier Housseaux, whose Web site had turned my life upside-down. With him was David Fell, the Squadron Association's Internet secretary who had flown over from England. At the hotel we met another Frenchman and a French lady who played important roles in making our two-day visit a tremendous adventure. Joachim Lelongt, a fighter pilot in his early thirties, had worked closely with Housseaux to organize an exciting, emotion-packed program. Mademoiselle Josselyn (Jo) Lejeune-Pichon had traveled from west of Paris to add enthusiasm and sparkle to the group.

*The Reims police report of the crash of D-Donald.*

The following morning we met Patrick Jonneaux and his wife, Monique. They had driven from Paris so that Patrick, who spoke fluent English, could be our interpreter. For the next two days the eight of us did everything and went everywhere together.

The first day's activities began with a visit to the crash site. The emotional impact was intense as I stood where my crew had died. Everyone was silent as I gazed into the clear blue sky where sixty years before there had been such horrendous violence. For a moment I looked to this hallowed spot of Mother Earth, then saluted the memory of my six friends who had surrendered their young lives that freedom might prevail. Several times that day, Olivier Housseaux said, "Because of you, our skies are clear!"

Just then a car pulled up and an elderly man got out and walked toward us. He introduced himself as Geoyet Gamotel. He told us how, as a twenty-one-year-old, he and some others had taken the bodies of my fellow crew members to the nearby village of Lavannes. I had goose bumps as I shook his hand and then embraced him! (A few months later, Joachim Lelongt found the police report of the crash in the local archives, dated March 13, 1943. It states that only one body was found in the wreckage of the fuselage. The other five bodies had been ejected. Wreckage was scattered over a large area. The explosion must have been much more

*Saluting at the crash site (left). Standing with Geoyet Gamotel. As a twenty-one-year-old he helped carry the bodies of my crew mates to a nearby village (right).*

*X marks the spot where I landed by parachute beside the railroad tracks (left). And standing at the spot in 2003 (right).*

violent than I had thought. Had any of my crew been conscious as they plummeted through the air to their deaths?)

We then drove to the nearby railway line, where I was able to identify the place where I landed by parachute. I had four clues: an embankment I had run down, the small copse of trees at the bottom, a bend in the otherwise straight railway line, and a steep incline which slowed a freight train sufficiently for me to jump aboard. Only one place had all four features. Here was another amazing situation which made it a fantastic day for me.

The main afternoon event was the memorial service at the Lavannes churchyard. A group of about one hundred and thirty gathered at the village green before moving in procession to the church. A brass band of local musicians led the way, while a single-engine Tiger Moth, piloted by

*Mayor Dutartre opened the memorial service with a short, moving speech. He concluded by saying, "Here in our cemetery lie your six fellows. Each year we pay homage to them on November 11 and July 14, as we do to our compatriots. For us, they symbolize the supreme sacrifice given to ensure the liberty of our people. They are also good examples for the younger generation. May the flowers we lay on their graves be the symbol of our gratitude and the expression of our duty to remember."*

*Following the mayor's speech with the English translation he gave us*

Marie-france Maigrot, circled continually overhead. Several children, each carrying a long-stemmed red rose to be placed on the graves, followed the band. Mayor Dominique Dutartre, David Fell, and I walked behind the children, followed by the rest of the procession.

As we entered the churchyard I steeled myself to control my emotions. Now, after sixty years, I was standing where my six crewmates were buried. The last time I had been with them they had been living, vibrant. The following pictures tell the story of the solemn remembrance service at the war graves in the northwest corner of the graveyard of the historic Lavannes church.

After laying a wreath at each grave, I stepped back and saluted. The emotion was intense.

Laying a wreath at John Todd's grave

Mayor Dutartre and I laying on the gravesite a beautiful bouquet of flowers given by the village of Lavannes.

I had never before experienced such spontaneous kindness, courtesy, and generosity as Joan and I received while in the Reims area. We were treated like royalty.

Scattered all over France are hundreds of gravesites of bomber crews that were shot down. Like at Lavannes, the graves are tended, and visiting relatives of the fallen airmen are treated as we were. Olivier Housseaux

*Another emotional moment—holding a broken propeller, the only surviving piece of wreckage from D-Donald. The children quickly joined me when I asked them to.*

speaks for many French people when he told my wife, "Because of you our skies are clear." At the end of each of his Web site pages he has written, "If somebody remembers you, you will never die."

We will remember; we will never forget!

But more important by far is that we never forget the One who gave His life so that every person of every nation and race and people would be freed from the tyranny of sin and Satan's occupation—if only that person will believe in Him. We are all prisoners of war in a world usurped by the archenemy, and we long to be liberated. "Even so, come, Lord Jesus!" (Revelation 22:20, NKJV).

*An aerial photo of the village of Lavannes. The white arrow (left center) points to the graves. After the memorial service, Pascal Garnotel, a villager and private pilot, kindly took Joan and me for a flight around Lavannes.*

# IF YOU ENJOYED THIS BOOK, YOU'LL ENJOY THESE AS WELL

## Red Star Rising

*Sunshine Siu Stahl as told to Kay D. Rizzo.* Shao Zhao Yang's extraordinary vocal talent propelled her to fame as an opera star in Communist China. Though she considered herself a Seventh-day Adventist Christian, on stage she could forget her Adventist upbringing and the public humiliation and persecution her family endured at the hands of Chairman Mao's Red Guards. The memories of her name change, family exile, and "denunciation meetings" made her grateful for her new life of stardom. But what of her faith? Could she ever really forget?

0-8163-2122-1. Paperback.

## Rainbow Over Hell

*Tsuneyuki Mohri;* translated by Sharon Fujimoto-Johnson. Easily one of the most dramatic conversion stories you'll ever read, **Rainbow Over Hell** lets you see the horrors of World War II through the eyes of a Japanese youth who joined the resistance against the Americans and became an assassin. Saburo's eventual arrest and death sentence formed the backdrop for a life-altering encounter with another condemned Man who died long ago to secure his freedom.

0-8163-2134-5. Paperback.